MAMA GONE GEEK

MAMA GONE GEEK

CALLING ON MY INNER SCIENCE NERD TO HELP NAVIGATE THE UPS AND DOWNS OF PARENTHOOD

Lynn Brunelle

Roost Books
Boston 2014

Roost Books
An imprint of Shambhala Publications, Inc.
Horticultural Hall
300 Massachusetts Avenue
Boston, Massachusetts 02115
roostbooks.com

9 8 7 6 5 4 3 2 1

First Edition
Printed in the United States of America

♾ This edition is printed on acid-free paper that meets the American National Standards Institute z39.48 Standard.
♻ This book is printed on 30% postconsumer recycled paper.
For more information please visit www.shambhala.com.

Distributed in the United States by Penguin Random House LLC and in Canada by Random House of Canada Ltd

Designed by Daniel Urban-Brown

LIBRARY OF CONGRESS CATALOGING-IN-PUBLICATION DATA

Brunelle, Lynn.
Mama gone geek: calling on my inner science nerd to help navigate the ups and downs of parenthood / Lynn Brunelle.—First edition.
pages   cm
Includes bibliographical references and index.
isbn 978-1-61180-151-4 (paperback)
1. Brunelle, Lynn—Family. 2. Parenthood—Humor. 3. Families—Washington (State)—Bainbridge Island. 4. Suburban life—Washington (State)—Bainbridge Island. I. Title.
HQ755.8.B77 2014
306.874—dc23
2014005578

For Kai and Leo—the very beings that put me on the Mama map. That said, I could never have done it without my adorable husband, Keith, coauthor in this life. This book is for him, too.

CONTENTS

INTRODUCTION
MOST PERSISTENT CAMPER

The summer before my fourth grade year was when I learned the truth about myself: I was a geek. I was a nerd.

Did I already have a fascination for science at that age? Hardly. At least I didn't think so. Science sucked. Everyone knew it. Everyone said so. To me science was a yawn. It was those lame kits at school, like boxed headaches, with corks and pebbles and questions like "What floats?" Duh. I was no science fan at age nine. But was I a geek? Hell yes. And that summer I was about to learn my first lesson that I still carry with me and will hopefully pass forward to my own kids.

Every year, from first grade through high school, when summer tumbled out of spring, I was bound for Camp Ketcha. It was a place of ceremony and of many firsts for me.

At the start of that summer—like every other—we stumbled off the bus, full of anticipation. Summer was here! We dropped our bags in a heap and gathered around the flagpole in a large circle. We were all decked out in blue shorts and white T-shirts with a navy pine tree and the words CAMP KETCHA emblazoned on our budding chests. Our heads were topped with blue Gilligan hats to keep the Maine sun from burning us fuchsia.

1

We sang songs, raised the flag, endured a morning pep talk and announcements, and were then sprung free to run in the fields, swim in the tea-brown pond, create macramé and papier-mâché treasures, or spend time at the horse stable.

The horse stable!

Our days were organized into chunks: the chunk I lived for was my time with the horses. I loved every one of those horses. Spicer, with his round, bronze belly, was perfect for riding bareback. Roper was rust-colored sass. He loved carrots, and if you weren't experienced, he'd take off running with you on his back. Dipper was long and lanky, brown, with a white diamond on her forehead.

Every hour of every day I made sure my counselors were aware that I had an *appointment* for the horses and that they were never to forget that I was *going* riding and "What time is it?" and "Is it time yet?"

My zeal for the horses was known camp-wide. There were chuckles and rolling eyes exchanged among the counselors, who didn't realize I'd noticed, when I insisted upon knowing the time and "Exactly how much longer until my riding lesson?"

I didn't care. I had my passion. I was determined to learn everything about these magnificent beasts. I spent hours in the library after camp looking at books about horses. I delved into the *how* and the *why* of horses. I found the angular curve of the tuber calcis, where the tibia and fibula ended and cascaded down to the hock and metatarsals, beautiful beyond words. The way the forelocks fell so gracefully over the bony occiputs at the tops of their skulls took my breath away. I just could not pass a horse without reaching out to pat the deltoid tuberosity rounding down from its shoulder. I studied their evolution, dazzled by the fact that fifty-five million years ago they were cat-sized creatures and stunned that their hooves are actually single toes upon which they balanced so steadily.

I knew about diseases that could plague them, from fluid-filled wind puffs that blemish the ankles to hoof-inflaming founder. I made discoveries about their perspective and wide range of vision because of their role in the predator/prey world.

I shared all this with anyone who seemed faintly interested—oftentimes mistaking dazed silence for fascination.

I curry-combed and dandy-brushed each animal to a sheen. I volunteered to shovel poop. I could even tell you the exact course the hay took to get there! I volunteered to help teach the little kids about horses. I could not get enough.

At the end of every day, we would once more circle the flagpole, my shirt dusty and me happily reeking of the barn. The sun slanted long, making our shadows reach into the tall grass beyond the "circle" area. We sang "Taps" as the flag was lowered, and we were all asked by our camp leader to think of the things that we were most grateful for that day: friends, fresh air, and a place to play. I would whisper to myself "horses."

On the final day of camp, tear-stained and exchanging addresses, hugs, and promises, we gathered for the last circle. I said my goodbyes to Roper and Spicer and Dipper, having clipped a piece of each horse's mane to keep.

The counselors gathered and handed out awards. We all had our hopes. Best All-Around Camper? Best Swimmer? Funniest Camper? Most Popular? I coveted the Best Horseback Rider award, of course, but knew in my heart that Patty or Amy, who were older and better, would win that. When my name was called, I stood up. The counselors were smiling. They bestowed upon me my award certificate:

Most Persistent Camper.

What was *that*? What did that *mean*? There was no mention of horses, sports, or popularity.

People clapped. Adults laughed and cheered. Sally, the mean girl, turned to me and whispered, "Horse nerd."

I brought my award home and showed my parents.

They laughed, tears flowing from their eyes.

"*What* does it mean?" I asked. "What *does* it mean? What does it *mean*?"

Every time I asked, my tone heightened—and their laughter increased.

I looked it up on my own in the fifty-pound dictionary in Dad's study.

Persistent:

1. Refusing to give up or let go; persevering obstinately.

2. Insistently repetitive or continuous: *a persistent ringing of the telephone.*

3. *Botany* Lasting past maturity without falling off, as the calyx on an eggplant or the scales of a pine cone.

4. *Zoology* Retained permanently, rather than disappearing in an early stage of development: *the persistent gills of fishes.*

For a while, I was embarrassed by this award. People had laughed at me. The word *nerd* seared into my self-confidence and made me shrink. Then the stubborn obstinacy I had been awarded for kicked in: *What's so bad?* I wondered. I had no clue how it had anything to do with Camp Ketcha, but I liked the part about not giving up. If being persistent meant to love something enough to want to learn everything about it, then bring it on.

What I did not yet know was that being Most Persistent Camper followed being passionate and was the foundation of curiosity, knowledge, and discovery. My persistence was a symptom of my exploration of passion and science.

Yes. Passion *and* science.

Before then, and for many people, it seems, science is something to be endured. It's that horrible frog dissection. It's the painful memorization of an endless list of weird words, compounds, and equations. It's knowing your Golgi bodies from your endoplasmic reticulum, your NaCl (salt) from your $C_{12}H_{22}O_{11}$ (sugar), and your $A= \prod R^2$ from your $E=MC^2$—all promptly forgotten once the test is over.

For others, like me, science has become the stardust that makes common things glow. The more you look, the deeper you dig, the brighter the sparkle. And for kids, it can be magical.

Isn't it remarkable when you hear crickets chirping on a summer night? It isn't simply a lovely sound. If you count the chirps per minute you can measure the temperature. Isn't it fascinating that because of the fact that all water molecules on the planet are finite we sip the very same water that dinosaurs did millions of years ago?

So I am today, still the persistent camper. I am a nerd, a geek, if you will, and happy to own it. While I tried to deny the title in my cool-seeking youth, I embrace it fully now.

My curiosity and love of throwing myself deeply into things remain strong. It's the core of who I am. My pleasure is to observe, experiment, fail, try again, laugh, and learn. It's with this core, geek or nerd or whatever you want to call it, that I navigate this life.

It's also a great way to approach the chaos and unpredictability of parenting. Not only for the sake of my own limp-along journey but also for my wonderful and patient husband, Keith, and our two sons, Kai and Leo, who are experiencing life and science more and more each day.

The art of science is observing, experimenting, making mistakes, solving problems, and delighting in the results. The inner nerd in all of us is the person who persists in reveling in the simple and not so simple things. That inner nerd is gleefully passionate about experiencing the one exhilarating ride we have on this planet.

Today, I am enchanted by the complexities and constructions of the universe. It makes the mundane magnificent. I don't just clean the house. I marvel over the dust particles lofted from dry African riverbeds and carried through the atmosphere to land on bookshelves half a world away. That and some dust mites and dead skin flakes that will make you keep the floor clean even when your eyes are bleary from lack of sleep.

This is curiosity and wide-eyed wonderment. The more you ask, the more you know. The more you know, the more you wonder. The more you wonder, the more beautiful the ride.

When I brought my passion for science into my parenting, it began to make all the difference to me and my kids.

This book is by no means a how-to. It is simply a how-I-do. My heart lifts when my boys are elbow deep in mud searching for crystals, when I catch them debating whether a chicken is related to a dinosaur, and when they're wondering about the force their jaws actually exert on jawbreakers.

Not a day goes by that the kids aren't engaged in a "Why," "What if," or "I wonder." It sharpens their sense of amazement and accessibility of knowledge while creating a broader view of themselves and the world.

To help encourage this sort of curiosity and wonder, I've included some of our favorite activities, projects, and experiments at the end of each chapter. I think they're fun. They also work as wonderful springboards into conversations that go even deeper. I know. It's a little geeky.

Geekiness is a treasure. It is a legacy that I love sharing, and one I hope Kai and Leo will pass along to their children someday.

Science isn't just for geeks. It's the future. If you're a parent or are planning to become one, it's your future.

1

YOUR CHLOROPHYLL IS SHOWING

IT'S NOT EASY BEING GREEN

WE WERE BRAND-NEW PARENTS alive with the green glow of possibility and giddy with a lack of sleep. We couldn't wait to share with Kai and Leo all the ideals of living a creative, sustainable life-style—embracing the joys of compost piles, locally grown, organic, fair trade, recycled, repurposed, and small-carbon-footprint living that we were seeing all around us. Kai was three and Leo was just a year old, but we felt it wasn't too early to start. It's never too early, right? We could imprint upon them the importance of being green as we embraced it ourselves.

We needed to move.

We were bursting at the seams of our little tall-skinny house on a postage stamp in Seattle. We had made the back driveway into a deck with a potted plant garden. We were itching to expand, and we were daring to look wide.

Keith had suggested Bainbridge Island across the sound. When we went over to take a look we found houses with yards. Big yards that were peppered with homes for bees, magnificent flower displays, gardens of trailing heirloom squashes, tomatoes, and herbs. Yards with chickens and coops designed by architects. All across town we found bus stops that were encrusted in moss and fern, farms that boasted organic non-GMO produce, and well-maintained trails that danced hikers past vistas unchanged since before our country even had a name. We found woods where old-growth trees stretched skyward and beaches that afforded views of mountains covered in snow reaching up from the horizon. Eagles soared through the skies. Deer gently munched at the sides of roads. Blackberries entwined the edges of paths everywhere, freely offering their dark, sweet delights.

When we made the move, we learned that the neighbors here didn't have Tupperware parties: they extended invitations to explore natural cleaning products that had no off-gassing. They had trail-maintenance parties. They painted outdoors. They hiked or biked or kayaked. They sold baggies in adorable patterns made of washable organic cotton. They welcomed us with bags of wild field greens and chanterelles gathered from the forest.

Bainbridge was the Mayberry of our dreams, played out on a glorious green stage. It was mindful and artsy, and beautiful and green. We couldn't wait to embrace the lifestyle. We couldn't wait to share the joys of green living with Kai and Leo. We knew of the perils our planet was heading into, and we were ready to do our part. We were prepared to arm our babies with all the knowledge and mindfulness necessary to create an army of kindness and planetary awareness of the future. We were drunk on wholesomeness. We had no idea about the perils of being green and wholesome.

We were barely moved in when the Fourth of July and all of its hometown splendor rolled around. To celebrate our move no fewer than twenty relatives arrived to see the new place and to take in the festivities. Blow-up mattresses dotted the floors, taking the place of the boxes I was desperately trying to clear from every room. There were two not particularly aesthetically appealing campers in the driveway. We had four birthdays to celebrate in July (all of us were born in July), and our neighborhood was having a street BBQ and fireworks on the Fourth. But first there was the annual Rotary Auction to attend: an enormous yard sale thrown on the campus of the middle school. For months, residents of the island cleaned house and donated items to the Rotary, which organized and priced and readied the loot for sale. Hundreds of thousands of dollars were raised every year for community programs. Who could resist?

Acres of books, toys, clothes, furniture, housewares, and art supplies waited for perusal. The night before the sale you could have a prelook, so you could know what you were aiming at. Keith and I were blown away by the hugeness of it. There were at least thirty-five Nordic Track machines lining one path. Twenty basketball hoops, golf clubs galore, and mountains of sports equipment. There were cars and boats and doors and windows and clothes and bikes and lawnmowers. The gym was dedicated to books. You could fill your bag for five dollars. This was heaven!

On the morning of July 3, the public waited silently as the national anthem warbled from the sound system. As soon as the last note was struck, the ropes were dropped and mayhem was unleashed into treasure land.

Keith and I left the kids with the extended family and proceeded to accumulate gently used items for our new house. We got ride-on horses on springs for the boys, metal Tonka trucks for the sandbox, a picnic table, jungle gym, coffee table, camp chairs, a deviled-egg plate, lamps, assorted candle molds, garden rakes, baseball bats, golf clubs, an antique typewriter, a desk, bags of books (good ones), a huge bag full of plastic dinosaurs, and woodcarving tools. We strapped it all onto a solidly built little red wagon and dragged it away, towering and teetering, to the applause and admiration of passersby.

That night, there was a street fair and a dance party downtown. The roads were roped off, and local bands dotted the streets with music and song. Kids drew with chalk. There were rides and slides. Families milled around and hailed each other from opposite sides of the bubbling street. People munched on tantalizingly delicious organic, locally grown satay sticks, fresh sushi rolls, crab cakes, and fresh berries. The sun shone. The mood was warm and welcoming.

The next day, we trundled downtown to watch a rather elaborate parade through the center of town. Anyone could enter, and many people did. This was not your ordinary marching-band-and-Girl-Scout-troop event—though they're included. In this parade, observers were treated to hula-hooping waitresses, Elvis look-alikes, Island quilting groups who marched with their creations mounted on wheeled frames, followed by an enormous toaster built around an old VW van trailed by a flurry of bakers dressed as huge pieces of (handmade, whole grain) toast from the local bakery. There was the Bainbridge Basset Hound Brigade—over twenty basset hounds dressed in hand-crafted costumes lumbering sprightly along at the ends of their handmade leashes. Not to be outdone, the corgis had their moment, as well as a handful of hamsters in wagons.

After the parade, teams of adult men dressed in vintage baseball uniforms battled it out in a game from yesteryear. There was hand-squeezed lemonade flavored with lavender. Fresh chocolate chip cookies and nitrate-free turkey dogs were available from cheery purveyors.

This was such a grand beginning! Keith and I were giddy. We really had found paradise. Our new hometown was rife with bright, peppy children of all ages and high-achieving mommies and daddies. We were ready to join ranks, no matter how exhausted or overwhelmed we already were. Island fever had us. Everything was possible. Everything was pure and beautiful! Our heads were spinning. The sun beat down. Sousa filled the air. The boys were crying. The dog bit a baseball player. It didn't matter. We had found our home, and we were launching headfirst into it.

After the fireworks blazed then fizzled and the company went home, we immediately rolled up our sleeves and got things rolling. We tilled the ground, edged it in driftwood and homemade birdhouses. We planted the garden. We set up a compost pile. For a whole month, it was bliss. Seeds pushed up through the well-fertilized dirt. I made viewing jars for the kids—we put paper towels and water in a mason jar with some beans and watched them sprout, marking their progress every day.

"Leaves shoot up and roots shoot down" became a little song we sang each time we looked at the jar. I was dazzled to tears by the roots-shoot-down verse as I relished the fact that we were setting down our own roots. Sigh.

The boys were dutifully amazed by the miracle of the sprouting seeds. They delighted in all things growing and green. Then came the day that they were even more transfixed with the raccoons and rats that showed up and fought savagely over the delights in our compost pile.

"Mommy, why is that big cat with the striped tail screaming like that?"

And "Mommy, our Sammy-cat brought in a pet mouse. It's a *big* one and it's running around the kitchen, leaving a trail of black rice."

These were not cute raccoons or rats. They were not Disney scalawags who played rascally tricks or helped clean up or make dresses. These were squealing, gnashing, scary vermin with untold viruses, bacteria, and parasites riding around on them. They were on my deck screaming, and in my house leaving rat poop trails like a twisted Hansel and Gretel.

This I was not embracing.

"What's wrong with the raccoons, Mom?" Kai asked as he pressed his nose up against the locked glass door to get a better look at the drama in the yard.

"Nothing is wrong with them, Honey, I am happy to live near them. But I don't want them coming too close."

"Why not?"

"They can be snarky, and they might bite, and they might have little bugs crawling on them that could jump on us and then crawl on us and nibble us."

"Yuck."

"Exactly."

We watched two raccoons hiss at each other. One had an apple core in its fist.

I was trying to figure out how to spin this.

"Let's kill 'em," Kai said, wielding a gun that he had fashioned out of a piece of toast.

I was horrified! Where did that come from?

"Honey! No making guns out of toast, and we are not going to kill them."

"But they're icky, Mom, and they could bite."

"Yes, but they have a right to be here, just like we do."

"Did they buy a house?"

"No. We kind of bought a house that was built near their home. And they seem to like what we are throwing away."

"Ew. Bang bang bang!"

We had our work cut out for us here.

I brought up the idea of a have-a-heart trap. Keith looked at me and smiled—rather patronizingly, I thought.

"What?"

"Think about it, Honey. You trap a raccoon and you trap a rat and then what?"

"Then YOU deal with it," I replied.

"OK. But where do we put them? Do we drive them to the peninsula, where they are viciously attacked by the native rodent population? Do we cart them off to the shore and hope they swim away? Do we bring them to the south part of the island and hope they don't make their way back here? Or—"

"OK, I get it. So what do we do?"

"You either Dr. Doolittle it and make friends, you Pa Ingalls it and we peg them with a shotgun and make our mark on our little prairie here, or we Darwin it and remove the food source and let them adapt, move away, or dare I say it—perish."

These were my choices. Natural selection. Them or us. There's something big at work here. I looked to Henry David Thoreau—another optimist who retreated to his cabin in the woods by Walden Pond. I could see him on Bainbridge. I imagined him, barefoot, cultivating his bean patch, waging war against the natural tenacious weeds that threatened to squeeze out the bean field interlopers should he not pick them out. Then he'd pause to lean on his hoe and soak in the "inexhaustible entertainment" of his environment, the sights and sounds of nature around him.

Yeah, what would he make of nasty, gnashing raccoons and ghastly rats?

Thoreau wasn't consumed with whether the year's crop succeeded or failed. He would note that the sun shines on plowed and fallow ground alike. Thoreau knew that part of every crop was a gift to the woodchuck. Weeds? No problem. Not for the birds at any rate. Thoreau was a roll-with-it kind of guy. He was all about accepting the blessings that nature bestowed upon him.

We opted for getting rid of the inviting compost pile. Guilt was beginning to skulk into my green ambitions. Some people could do this. I, it seems, could not.

This was just the beginning.

I tried cleaning the house with vinegar and baking soda and rags. It was hard to get over the pickle smell. We, as humans, have a strong associative memory with smell. To me, *clean* doesn't exactly smell like pickles. The Lower East Side of Manhattan smells like pickles. I like pickles, but I prefer my house to have a stereotypical lemony or pine-scented clean. Or worse—according to the natural-cleaning zealots— bleach. My definitive nongreen was starting to show.

I tried the simple cleansers. When the cat—who was upset about the move and the raccoons and the rats—started to pee in the corner of the dining room, I bought an all-natural pet-odor remover. I doused the area with it, lulled into a sense of safety from the "It really works!" claim on the label.

I discovered that it really *doesn't* work! I tried orange peel extract. I tried cat pheromones. *All-natural* cat pheromones.

Yuck!

I stopped. The dining room still smelled like a litter box—with hints of citrus and I don't know what. I finally tried bleach, and *boom*, the pee smell was gone.

"Mommy, this room smells like the pool," Kai said.

"It's bleach, Honey."

"It smells better than cat pee."

"Yes, it sure does."

I was totally a green fraud. I waited for the phone call telling me that the neighborhood watch had detected an enormous amount of off-gassing from my housecleaning products and I wasn't composting, so there had been a meeting and we were deemed unsuitable for the glorious life on Bainbridge. We must be kicked off the island.

The horror.

I redoubled my efforts. I looked online to find tips I could use and share with the boys about being green.

"Although it seems like a big task, green parenting can be fun and easy if you take the proper steps," one website assured me.

That sounded promising.

Reuseable diapers. They were first on the agenda. My shoulders sagged. I knew people did this. People who were much more mindful and kind and natural did this. The idea of it was fine—for other people. Surely this would waste water, and surely the devil bleach would have to come into play or we would all be suffering from bacterial infestation—right?

I had to skip this. I made an effort to buy diapers that would bio-degrade, and then we got a mortgage. On the diaper front we fell into Costco. Bulk diapers at a cheaper cost. I was single-handedly killing the planet.

Next?

Reuse. OK, the Rotary Auction. We were all about reusing! Maybe I wasn't such a lost cause.

Recycle. We had bins. I recycled. But when I read an article about a woman whose house and family were so efficient that she only had a twisty tie for a month's worth of living, I plunged into a dark green depth. Seriously? No matter what I did, I produced garbage. Now that I was on the anti-rat and raccoon binge, I was adding more scraps to the trash bin, making me even more intolerable.

Conserve energy. OK, I turn off lights and water. I was getting some-where now.

"Mom?" It was Kai and Leo. "Look!"

They were *covered* in grass stains. Keith had mown the lawn, and Kai and Leo had been rolling in the clippings. They smelled like a meadow. They looked like Martians.

"Leo and I are grassy green!"

My first thought was that I would have to use bleach on their clothes to get rid of these grass stains; but then I grabbed the reins.

"I have an idea. Let's go!" I told them, and we raced outside. I grabbed an old, white rag. It had a slight vinegar smell from clean-ing. We experimented with making it green by rubbing the grass. We squeezed, we pushed, and we even pounded that grass to break open its cells and spill out the glorious green. I told them about how plants are green because of chlorophyll and they used that very greenness to make food from the sun.

We do our best, don't we?

I had found my niche. My happy, green place. I had been so consumed with trying to fill a space full of unmet expectations of being the perfect mom, the perfect green citizen, the perfect *whatever* that I lost touch with what I really held dear. I took a page from my persistent camper days—look and look again and again from a variety of different angles. Delight in the basic. Savor the amazement of what's right there in front of you. Allow it to express itself and be there to witness it. Slow down, watch, and respect it (whatever *it* happens to be) for being as amazing as it is.

"Green is awesome!" Kai exclaimed.

Truer words have never been uttered.

LEAF SMASH T-SHIRT

Chlorophyll—the stuff that makes green plants green—is a great stain maker. Don't fight it; roll with it! Use it as a dye. Use a hammer and release a beautiful and permanent burst of chlorophyll to create a jaw-droppingly cool T-shirt. Or use a white pillowcase and make a dreamy, leafy pillow.

WHAT YOU NEED

- Fresh leaves (ferns, raspberry leaves, even herbs like parsley work really well)
- A white T-shirt
- Thin cardboard (the kind that comes in shirt packages works well, or use an old manila folder)
- Paper towels
- Hammer

WHAT YOU DO

1. Put a piece of cardboard inside your T-shirt so the stain won't soak through to the back.

2. Place the leaves on your shirt in whatever design you like.
3. Place a couple of paper towels over the leaves.
4. Carefully hammer over the whole leaf. You have to hammer the complete design or it won't show up on your T-shirt. Go around the edges, and make them as complete as possible.
5. When you're finished, remove the paper towels and lift off the leaves.
6. Keep it out of direct sun until you have a chance to set it as the sun will fade the design. To set the design toss the shirt in the dryer for 10 minutes.

TRY THIS!

Most plants will stain fabric, so use them to dye your shirt. Search around for interesting leaves and flowers and create your own designs.

2

WAIT A MINUTE, I'M EATING WHAT?

FROM THE TIME they were babies, I obsessed about food for the kids. I read all the books. I made my own baby food. Really, it wasn't all that hard: steam up veggies, throw them in a blender, pop the goo in ice cube trays, and freeze. It was easier than jars and tasted a whole lot better. I had also read that this was the way to get your kids to love real vegetables. I will say it worked—for a while. When Kai and Leo were little, they ate everything. They loved salmon and avocado and broccoli, kale, mango, squash, and quinoa. I know! It was impressive. I felt impressive.

I had my momentary feeling of smugness and superiority as a mama-of-the-year who would never have her kids ride the macaroni and cheese train. Sheesh!

My lesson (the one I *keep* learning): don't ever feel smug or superior when it comes to anything, because the tide always turns. Always! Was he three or four when Kai suddenly stopped eating cold sesame noodles, seaweed, kiwi, and blueberries? I can't remember. What I recall is the sudden change. He began to notice color and pick out molecules of the offending pigment, then hold them up to me like an accusation.

I decided to turn it into a color game. "Eat your rainbow!" I warbled. RedOrangeYellowGreenBlueIndigoViolet! ROY G. BIV is coming for dinner! Rainbow Roy! Let's eat him up!

This so didn't even begin to work. Kai cried and said he'd never eat a rainbow; that would make him sad. I tried to tell him the happiness of the rainbow would get inside and make him happy if he ate it. He asked if he could eat crayons instead.

I thought it would pass.

I *still* think it will pass. Let's just say boxes of mac and cheese have a permanent spot on our shelf. They're organic, at least.

Don't get me wrong. We tried the whole get-the-kids-interested-in-gardening-and-they-will-learn-to-love-real-food-because-they're-invested thing. Nope. We planted everything from kohlrabi and rutabagas to carrots and lettuce. They liked growing things. It was fun. They loved the seeds, the sprouts, the watering, but when it came to harvest time, both of them expressed horror that carrots were actually down there in the dirt, next to worms and bugs. They handily put two and two together and deduced that soil was also probably where worms and bugs pooped. Therefore, carrots *were* actually worm poop. *Carrots = worm poop* became a handy metaphor for all vegetables. They vowed never to let those nasty things pass their pristine lips.

That was kind of a bump in the road to living off the land.

When they discovered where eggs actually came *out* of a chicken, that was the end of morning scrambles. I could still get them to eat pasta sauce—I'd add ground turkey and puree every single available veggie to put in the sauce. They would get their daily five by hook or by crook. I knew we were in for a ride when they found vegetables offensive. What would they do when they learned that chicken was actually *chicken*?

Leo asked one day when we were eating chicken enchiladas.

"Where does chicken come from?"

"It's actually a chicken."

His eyes grew huge. "What?"

"Yup. The chickens that walk around and lay eggs and cluck and all that are raised by humans and cared for and when it's time, they are eaten."

"Wait just a minute! I'm eating WHAT? I am actually eating the body of a chicken?"

I held firm. "It lived a good life—"

"Oh Mom! DON'T! I can't know about this chicken? Was his name Fred? Did he watch TV? Did he do tricks?"

Both Kai and Leo spit out their enchiladas. They looked at me in horror.

"OK, boys. I understand what you're feeling. It's kind of weird. But as human beings, we depend on other species for food, so our bodies can grow and stay healthy. Everything is made up of molecules, and we need to keep putting molecules in our bodies to survive. We're just reorganizing the molecules. It's a fact of life. Every animal eats something."

"Like what? What did this poor chicken eat?"

"Truthfully? Scraps and grains and bugs—"

"Uck! BUGS?"

I pressed on. I ate my enchilada as an example. I believed I could weather this if I stayed calm. "Mmmm, this is good."

They both yelled, "MOM!"

"Some animals eat only meat—only the flesh of other animals. Like the dogs and the cats. They're carnivores."

"Mom, they eat pellets. Brown pellets."

"I know, Love; those pellets are made of meat."

"I will never look at Oggy the same way again," Kai sighed and glanced at Oggy, who wagged his tail.

"And some animals eat plants."

"And worm poop."

"Yum!"

"And what do plants eat?"

"Good question. They make their own food. They use the sun and the soil and they make sugars."

"So plants eat sunshine?"

"In a way, I guess! Yes. I kind of like that."

"Well, that's what I want to eat, too."

OK, now we were getting somewhere.

"You can."

"I can? How?"

"By eating your veggies and fruits and chicken and grains and all the yummy stuff I put in front of you every day. Everything comes from sunshine."

"How about ice cream?"

"Yup. Sunshine. Made of milk, which comes from cows that eat grass, which makes its food from sunshine."

A game. This could work.

"M&Ms!" Leo burst out with. A grin on his face. Kai smiled, too.

"Chocolate comes from cacao, which is a tree. The tree uses sun to make sugars."

"Pizza?"

"Tricky. The crust comes from wheat, which is a plant—the plant uses sun. Tomato sauce—tomatoes are plants. Cheese, milk, cow, grass, sun. Pepperoni . . ."

Uh oh.

"Comes from a pig . . ."

"A PIG?"

"The pig eats corn and the corn is a plant and the plant gets energy from sunshine. See?"

I blipped over pig. "We eat stuff. We eat plants and animals. We're not heartless about it, boys. If we feel thankful to the plants and animals, that's good, right?"

"I guess."

"Come on—who wants a bowl of sunshine?"

"Heath Bar crunch?"

"Perfect."

After that, the kids were still picky; but thanks to Huck Finn/Becky Thatcher Day, we were in for a big change.

On Bainbridge, in April, at the Sportsman's Club, Huck Finn/Becky Thatcher Day marks the opening of the fishing season. Kids gather from the island with bamboo poles and race to see who can catch the first, the biggest, or the most fish in a certain time period. It's another Mayberry moment here on the island.

Keith was excited to take the boys for their first fishing expedition. It was boys only. Bonding time. Keith and our neighbor Chip dug up worms with the boys the night before and readied the poles. The air was abuzz with adventure.

This was a big deal. This would be the first time Kai and Leo would be faced with taking the life of an animal to eat. I sensed there might be trouble brewing.

It's important for them to make that connection. Would the experience scar them? Turn them into vegans? I was prepared. I had recipe books. I had been a vegetarian for twelve years, until I became pregnant with Kai and was determined to make up for lost time and scarf down every hamburger I could find. I could do vegan. I had a blender. Life would be filled with purees and pasta. Doable.

I tucked them in that night and prepared them by talking about ancient hunting societies and how the prey was part of the ceremony. Keith chuckled at me. At dawn, I sent them off into the foggy morning armed with muffins, cocoa, worms, and solid thoughts. I choked back tears as Keith reassured me that they'd be fine.

Hours later, when they returned, I hugged them all and asked them how it went.

Immediately Kai and Leo yelled, "AWESOME!"

Keith and Chip were all grins.

"Kai caught the first fish!" Keith said proudly.

"The biggest one, too! I won a fishing pole with Batman on it."

"I caught five!" Leo piped in. "I got a pole, too!"

The boys were dancing. They were wet. They were mosquito-bitten and delighted with themselves.

"How was it, really?" I asked Keith. "Were they weirded out by it?"

"Show Mom," Keith said to the boys.

"It was like *this*, Mommy," Kai said. "I threw out my line and BAM! It was pulling me back. I grabbed my pole and ran up the bank dragging the pole with me."

Leo added, "Yeah and then the FISH came out. It was silver and flopping like this."

Kai and Leo dropped to the floor and writhed and twisted and flopped around and gurgled loudly.

"This is what the fish looked like when we dragged it out and tossed it on the bank!"

They both stood up laughing. "It was AWESOME! And then we said, 'Thanks, fish,' and now let's eat them."

What had changed? In one morning, the kids had embraced the predator-prey relationship and made their place in the whole scheme of things. Thank you, Huck Finn and Becky Thatcher. All Kai and Leo needed to do was apply it to their own reality. Hmm. Food for thought.

The kids were fine. Together they had caught ten fish and won two fishing poles—one with Batman on it—as well as a new passion for catching fish and evidently eating them. We fried them that evening. The boys gobbled up the fish and left the green beans on the plate.

It was a start.

TRACE IT BACK

- Take any food item and trace it back to the sun. Take pizza for example. The dough is made from wheat, which is a plant that uses the sun to grow.
- Cut out pictures of food from magazines and draw pictures showing how it is traced back to the sun.
- Create a mobile with the sun as the centerpiece.

MAKE A PIZZA SAUCE OR SALSA GARDEN

Take it a step further and set aside part of a garden or pot to grow something from scratch—like salsa or pizza sauce and toppings.

WHAT YOU NEED
- A few pots or a section of the garden set aside
- Seeds, such as tomato, herbs, onion, garlic cloves

WHAT YOU DO
1. Plant the seeds according to the directions on the package.
2. Watch them sprout.
3. Harvest and eat!

3

I'LL SHOW YOU MINE

LULU AND KAI HAD BEEN BEST FRIENDS since they were three. They always had a lot of fun together. They made puppet shows, painted, ran around, bounced on the trampoline, climbed trees, laughed, danced, ate cupcakes—and then one day they took off all their clothes.

I knew the day would come. Kai was fascinated with his body. We sang songs about elbows, knees, and other joints. He loved the names of bones and was enchanted by calling his bum the gluteus maximus. Kids are curious. They are innocent, and they are explorers.

I was still surprised.

"Mom, did you know that Lulu has a 'china and no penis? No penis!" Kai announced one day when we were driving.

He was shocked. I think he thought all kids would have one because he did.

"Yup." I was treading lightly. "Girls have an 'innie' and boys have an 'outie.'"

"Yeah, but that's weird. I know moms don't have penises, but—"

"Well, Kai. Lulu is a girl, after all. And it's not sad that she doesn't have a penis. It's cool! Girls get to grow the babies inside their bodies, if they want to. That's super cool."

"Maybe, but not as super cool as having a penis!"

"They're both cool, Honey."

Was I really saying this out loud?

"Mom?"

"Yeah, Love?"

"Remember that guy on the ferry with only one eye?"

Where was this going? "Yes."

"He said he lost his eye in an accident. Is that what happened to Lulu?"

"No, Sweetie. She was born that way. Girls are different than boys. They're born different. Girls have different organs inside their bodies than boys. Here's the thing. Bodies are beautiful. But, boys and girls are different. Did you know when babies are very tiny inside their mom, they all look the same at first?"

"They do?"

"Sort of. Girl babies have two X signs that give directions to become a girl, and boys have an X and a Y sign that give directions to make a boy."

"That's not the *same*, Mom."

"I know, but when the babies are tiny and the parts are all starting to take shape—parts like elbows, ulnas, femurs, skulls, and ears and stuff—"

"And 'chinas and penises."

"Yeah . . . babies look alike at first. After about six weeks, if the baby is made with a Y sign, then things start to change. Chemicals are in the blood, and boy parts get made."

"It starts the same and ends up different?"

"Yup. Just like everything, really. All people start the same, but in the end we're all different. Isn't that amazing? It's all normal. It's all good."

"Different is good?"

"Oh, yeah! If everyone were the same, wouldn't it be pretty boring?"

"I guess, maybe."

"People come in all different sizes, shapes, and colors. It's what makes life as a human interesting."

I could feel a teachable moment coming on, and I couldn't stop it. Conditions were perfect. We were in the car, on our own, and we had a ways to go.

"Think about it. Even hair color. Kolya has brown hair, you have black hair, Olivia has red hair, and Liz has silver hair."

"It's all hair, but it's all different."

"Yup, and we humans come in all sorts of shapes and sizes, don't we?"

"Uncle Bill's tall, and you're not."

"Yup."

"And Daddy has big, strong shoulders."

"Yes, he does."

"And Popo's round, and Cindy's tall and thin."

"That's right, and some people have black skin, tan skin, reddish skin, pink skin, white skin, and even bluish skin."

"Really? Bluish skin?"

"Sometimes! And some people can't walk as well as others. And some people don't have the same number of fingers or toes or arms or legs. Some people talk in a different way. Some people can't see or hear or talk, but we're all connected and we're all alike because we're people."

"And not all of them have penises, right, Mom? But that's OK. Right?"

"Yes, Love. Only the boys do, and that's just fine!"

"Mom?"

"Yes, Love?"

"Do giraffes start out the same as people and end up as giraffes?"

"Kind of. They start off with a giraffe cell from the mom, and one from the dad. They come together and there's a code that tells the cells what to become. That part's the same—two cells coming together—for everything from bats, kangaroos, and polar bears. But people couldn't have a giraffe, and cows don't have kittens. You know?"

"Do those all come in boy and girl versions, too?"

"Yup."

Kai started laughing. He laughed so hard he couldn't breathe. When he calmed down I asked him, "What is so funny, Bug?"

"Giraffe penises. I never thought of that before. It's funny!"

It kind of is.

We drove in silence for a while.

"Honey?"

"Yes, Mom?"

"When it comes to Lulu, I know you are both curious and that's OK. But you have to be respectful and never touch."

"OK, Mom."

I thought the curiosity was satisfied, and I thought I had used it as a route into diversity and acceptance, and I thought I had safely navigated the Lulu-Kai exploration show. I was feeling smug.

Hah!

I was wrong. The next day as Lulu's mom, Ivy, and I were talking in the driveway of preschool after picking up the kids, they had hopped into our car and waited for us. We happened to glance in, and they were giggling and naked!

It was all very innocent, but now new rules needed to come into play. Should I be heavy-handed? I didn't want him to feel weird about the whole thing. I didn't want to associate curiosity and differences with shame. I wanted to do this difficult dance right.

I had another opportunity that weekend. We were invited over to Lulu's house for a family dinner.

"Here's the thing, Bud," I lectured Kai in the car on the way. "What is important to remember when playing with Lulu?"

"I know, I know. We're all different and some people have one eye and some don't have penises."

Keith looked at me sideways and whispered, "What?"

I breathed.

"*Who* has only one eye and no penis?" Leo asked. He was shocked.

"Hang on hang on hang on. You're right. All people are different, and yet we're all the same."

"Because we're *all* people."

"Yeah, but I have *two* eyes *and* a penis," added Leo. He was still confused.

"Yes you do, Leo, but let's get back to family rules when playing with people."

"We know, we know. Play nice. Include everyone," Kai said dutifully.

"And . . ." I urged.

"And keep my clothes on."

"OK, great," I said. Keith snickered and shook his head.

Dinner was a delight. The kids took off to watch a movie in Lulu's parents' room. Keith and I and Lulu's mom and dad had an awesome playdate. We laughed. We were nice. We included everyone, and *we* kept our clothes on.

No one was prepared for what happened next.

The quietness struck all the adults at the same time, and I laughed casually.

"I'll check on them!" I said. I had noticed Lulu a short while before sneaking over by the front door and grabbing something. She had the cutest, most impish nature. I really didn't think much of it. I had grinned conspiratorially at her. She had grinned at me and disappeared into the bedroom with all the kids. That was a half hour ago.

When I strolled to the room, I heard shrieks of laughter. The door was ajar. I knocked and said, "How are all you chickens doing in here?"

They answered with clucks, more laughter. I opened the door to reveal Leo, buck naked, jumping on the bed. Kai turned to me—he was fully clothed and made up like a farsighted drag queen. He had lipstick artfully placed *all* over his face—eye shadow lipstick, lips WAY out of the lines, blush. Even drawn-on lipstick earrings.

"Hi, Mommy!"

"Whoa . . . wh-wha-what's going on?" I asked as gently as I could muster.

Leo also was lipsticked all over, with circles and tribal markings over every inch of him.

He bounced enthusiastically on the bed and announced, "I'm eating mints!"

Lulu grinned in the corner. She was fully clothed and held the lipstick. The contents of her mom's purse were strewn over the bed. I looked at Lulu and Kai. My jaw dropped.

"Kai!"

"What, Mom?"

"What's on your face?"

"Lulu made me over. She used lipstick."

I looked at Lulu.

She concentrated on the tube. "B-E-R-R-Y C-R-U-S-H!" she read.

"Berry Crush, huh?"

"I made him over in Berry Crush."

"Berry Crush, Berry Crush, Berry Crush," Leo chanted as he bounced, smelling of Altoids.

I turned to Kai. "You know the rules, Kai!"

"Yeah I do! And we did it! We *included* everyone *and* kept *our* clothes on!"

He smiled.

Lulu, with an impish grin, nodded proudly.

Leo spun around and showed me his bum. It, too, was covered in lipstick. "Lulu says these are lips, too!"

"Leo, that's your gluteus maximus," Kai said flatly.

I looked at Lulu. She smiled. "Berry Crush!" she whispered.

The three of them collapsed in giggles.

My mouth was open. The kids kept on jumping and giggling. How do I handle this without freaking out the kids, the parents, or myself? I couldn't do it on my own. I had to have the others see what I was witnessing.

I returned to the dining room. Keith saw the look on my face.

"What is it?" he said.

"All I can say is Berry Crush. We owe you new lipstick, Ivy. You have to see this for yourselves. Technically, Kai and Lulu followed the rules."

Luckily, we all thought it was funny; but secretly I was mortified.

We grabbed the kids and took them home. As Leo soaked in a tub, I constructed a zillion apology notes to Lulu's mom in my head.

I'm sorry my child decorated his brother's gluteus maximus with your elegant lipstick.

No.

I'm sorry my child bounced naked on your bed and ate your mints.

Nope.

Berry Crush sure is a pretty shade. . . .

No.

Did you know lipstick doesn't wash off easily?

Nuh-uh.

I'm sorry I didn't know how to handle this whole situation.

Nothing seemed appropriate.

In the end I offered the family a new tube of Berry Crush, some washable body paint, and a promise that the scene would never repeat. It was the best I could do.

Lulu and Kai are still friends, and our families are still very close. When the mention of Berry Crush comes up, all we do is laugh and sigh and laugh again.

As parents, we walk a fine line between wanting to keep things open, stress-free, full of joy, wonder, and respect. Bodies are beautiful. OK to look, but don't touch. People are different. It's all good. We want to celebrate the body and all its differences; but when it comes right down to it, I guess it's OK to simply draw the line—but not in lipstick!

💡 HOMEMADE WASHABLE BODY PAINT

Humans have been adorning themselves with painted body designs since caveman days. A stripe here, a spiral there, or a few faux claw marks can really make a statement. It's fun! But it's not fun if it doesn't come off and you have to send your kid to school with orange whiskers and a forehead dotted with purple triangles. Here's a workable—and washable—solution.

WHAT YOU NEED

- Nontoxic tempera paint (washable)
- Clear, nontoxic, all-natural detergent or shampoo
- Containers for each paint color

WHAT YOU DO

1. Decide what colors of body paint you want to make. Choose a jar for each color.
2. Mix nontoxic tempera paint with all-natural hand wash or shampoo until you achieve the desired color.

3. Paint!
4. Wash!
5. Discard any homemade body paints over thirty days old.

MAKE IT EDIBLE

You can make delicious body paint with yummy ingredients.

- Mix just enough corn syrup with cocoa to create a beautiful brown body paint that is also edible.
- Mix one part corn syrup to four parts confectioner's sugar, plus as much food coloring as required to obtain the color that you want. Add a bit of flavored extract, such as maple or almond, or sprinkle some ground cinnamon in to make your edible body paint even tastier. Be aware that even though you can eat it, food coloring can stain!

4

I HATE TO TELL YOU, BUT YOU'RE A LITTLE BIT FAT

DID YOU KNOW that a person who weighs 120 pounds on earth would weigh just eight pounds on Pluto? Not that I've seen 120 pounds since I was in, like, seventh grade; but it's nice to know it's just a number and that the mass of me is a variable. There's comfort in that. The kind of comfort I clung to when we packed for Hawaii.

Isn't it so boring to hear moms complain about their soft figures since they had "the baby"? It is. But I am no exception. I complain. I worry about it. I joke about it to deflect the niggling worry that I am no longer an attractive, young thing. I am now married and saddled with a ring of blubber around the middle that, like a life preserver, just won't quit.

I know, I know. In my head, I am good. I own my body.

It has taken me years of fending off obsession and diets and slimming jeans and shape-wear and vertical stripes and slimming shades of color. I swim. I walk. I am strong. I am still working on the self-image stuff.

So when Kai was three and a half and Leo was one and a half, and we were packing for Hawaii, I had to face the idea that I would be mostly nude in public. (Lycra does not a cover-up make.) The pools, the great bodies of water that were my friends during pregnancy, were now staring me in the face. I worried.

But it was Hawaii, after all. Paradise. Plenty of real bodies, from poi-eaters to Midwest corn-fed mamas. I was *not* unique. I had emerged from the hotel—pale-skinned "shark bait," as Keith called me—in my new suit that I hoped was slimming. I felt faux-confident as I walked across the pool deck in the early morning warmth. I had an iced coffee under my belt and was feeling good. The pool was sparsely attended at that hour of the morning. I decided to take the leap, both metaphorically and literally. To hell with this body insecurity. It's ridiculous!

I passed the waterfalls, the koi pond, the large main pool, and the grotto hot tubs and made my way to the small pool off to the beach side of the pool complex, where Keith and the boys were splashing in the shallows. I didn't skip a beat. I dropped my towel, sprinted up the stairs, and leapt into the waterslide. It was exhilarating! I zipped and dropped and turned and finally shot out like a buttered ham in a cannon, landing with a splash.

I rose to the surface laughing and floated over to Kai. He was laughing and smiling at me. He reached for me as he scrambled to get close. This boy was so sweet—love in his eyes. Here we were, in paradise.

"Mommy?"

"Yes, Love?" I reached over and cupped his freckled cheek.

"I hate to tell you, but you're a little bit fat."

How can a single sentence undo a woman's confidence so thoroughly?

I immediately started sobbing. It wasn't my finest moment. Kai's face crumpled and he looked at me in shock. He started to sob.

Keith thought we were drowning, so he lunged to us both and tried to drag us out.

This made me cry harder, and sent Kai into hysterics.

Leo, who was in Keith's arms, was startled; so he began to sob, too.

"What's wrong? *What's* wrong? What's *wrong*?" Keith erupted in rapid succession.

This made us all cry even more.

It was ugly.

I handed Kai off to Keith and hauled myself from the pool. He stood there, confused, a sobbing boy under each arm. I wrapped the towel around myself and folded into a chaise just in time for the waitress—who was wearing a bikini—to come by and ask if she could get me a drink.

It was 6:30 in the morning!

"Piña colada, please," I mustered.

"Of course," she said with a wide, island smile.

She walked off, and I found myself again.

Wait, wait, wait just a second. When did I get pathetic?

I hailed her.

She turned.

"Can you make that an iced tea, please?"

She smiled. "Of course."

I dropped my towel and hopped into the pool. I wrapped my arms around my sobbing boys. I picked up Kai and looked him in the eye.

"MOMMY! I'm SORRRRRRRRRRRRRRRRY!" he sobbed.

"Sweetie, you just surprised me. That's all. I know I may seem a little bit fat, and yes, it's interesting how a woman's body responds to getting older. . . ." I really had no idea where I was going. I wanted to let him know fat isn't anything to be ashamed of. I wanted to arm him with all the things with which I really wanted to arm myself.

"Tell me what happened," Keith was calmer now.

"I came out of the slide and Kai said, 'I hate to tell you, but you're a little bit fat,' and I lost my cool."

"Oh Sweetie, that's a line from the movie we watched this morning at 4:00 when they got up because of jet lag. A bug said it to a cater-pillar. Kai thought it was funny. He's been saying it ever since. You should have seen the bikini waitress's response. Did you *see* her? Not fat!"

I looked at Keith. We both broke out in hysterics.

Then I looked at Kai.

"In the movie it was funny, Mommy. I don't think you are fat. I think you are beautiful!" Kai launched at me, wrapping his small body around me, clinging and sobbing again.

"Oh, baby. I didn't know it was a line from a movie. I did wonder why you delivered it in a German accent, though. You are funny. I just misunderstood. I was only thinking from my perspective, and I was feeling a little vulnerable. The great thing is you brought it to my attention that I was worried about something I should not spend time worrying about. Right?"

"Huh?"

"Well, if I am worried that I need to make my body more fit, I shouldn't cry about it. I should just do something about it. You helped me see that!"

"I did?"

"Yup."

"Hey, Mom," he said, and pushed off into the pool. "Watch me swim." He swam out four strokes and then back.

"Well done! Watch me float." I floated, belly up.

"Wow! How do you do that?"

"Well, Honey, believe it or not, I am an awesome floater because . . . I'm a little bit fat!"

He looked at me, wide-eyed; he looked like he could fall on either side of my joke.

Thankfully, we both laughed.

"Daddy floats, too!"

"Yup."

"REALLY well!"

"Happily, yes."

"Hey!" Keith said and splashed us.

Dive in. That's what this was telling me.

"What else floats?"

Kai climbed out of the pool and amassed a few objects. A quarter, a container of sunscreen, goggles, a coffee cup. One by one, he dropped things in the pool and exclaimed every time something either sank or floated. If it floated, he bellowed, "It's a little bit fat!"

This was the mantra of the whole trip. Delight expressed if something floated. Joy when something was a little bit fat.

It was a good lesson for me to learn.

After a poolside lunch of sushi, I had an idea. I took my water bottle and a packet of soy sauce and brought it back to the pool. We filled up the bottle with pool water and dropped the soy sauce packet in. It floated. We capped the bottle and then squeezed. The packet sunk. When we let go, it floated.

"It's a little fat, and then not!" Kai exclaimed. His eyes lit up. "Like you, Mommy!"

"You are right about that, Honey."

"But how does that work?"

"It's all about density."

Truer words have never been uttered.

"What?"

"Well, the soy sauce itself would sink in the water, but it's in a packet. It has a little pocket of air that holds it up. See it?"

"Oh, I see it. Is it like a little balloon that makes it float?"

"Exactly. When you squeeze the bottle, you squeeze the soy sauce packet and you make the air bubble smaller and it just can't hold the packet up any more."

"Because of pressure?"

This metaphor was biting me right on the blubbery butt! "Yep. Under that kind of pressure, it will sink."

"Hmm." Kai trotted off and hopped into the pool with his bottle. He squeezed that thing and let it go all day. Up-down-up-down-up-down. He explained it to anyone who walked by. All trip.

Yes, there was part of me that was dazzled by the fact that my boy was geeking out over a physics experiment; but every time I saw Kai's delighted surprise and amazement at the ups and downs, I reminded myself that once again, my salvation was in science.

It's all about floating and sinking, isn't it? We put pressure on ourselves and the little bubble that holds us up is overwhelmed, and we sink. Let go a little, and we rise back up to the top. We're so used to being programmed to believe and be what we are told: be skinny, be fit, always smile, have perfect hair in all the right places (not the wrong ones).

Life isn't always that easy. We all have moments when we sink and moments when we float. Moments when we're a little bit fat. And moments when we just believe that we are. I guess the trick is to be clear-eyed and just enjoy the constant dance between the floating and the sinking.

⚡ SOY SAUCE SINKER ⚡

Make a pop bottle Cartesian diver that shows when you increase pressure and squeeze the bottle, the packet of soy sauce inside sinks. Let go and it rises. (Kind of what we do to ourselves! We put pressure on ourselves and sink. Let go a little and we rise back up to the top.)

WHAT YOU NEED

- A plastic soda pop bottle with labels removed
- Cap
- Water
- Small metal paperclips
- Unopened soy sauce packet (ketchup or mustard packets work well, too)

WHAT YOU DO

1. Put a metal paperclip on your soy sauce packet.
2. Fill your pop bottle with tap water, leaving an inch or two empty at the top.
3. Place the packet in the water. It should float just below the surface. If it rises above the water line, then add a second paperclip.
4. Cap the bottle, and close it tightly.
5. Squeeze the bottle in the middle. You may need to give it a really good squeeze.
6. Watch the packet drop. (If you are squeezing like crazy and nothing happens, take out the packet and add another paperclip.)
7. Let go, and watch the packet rise.

WHAT'S GOING ON?

It's all about pressure. When you squeeze the bottle, you compress the little air pocket in the soy sauce packet and it can't hold up the packet anymore so it sinks. When you let go, the air springs back to normal and the soy packet rises.

5

LIZARD BRAIN

REMEMBER SISYPHUS? He was the Greek guy condemned for the rest of eternity to roll a huge boulder up a hill, and just at the point when he succeeds in getting it to the top, it rolls back down to the place where it started.

Keith has his Sisyphean moment every spring, when he decides that this is the year we will have grass growing in the side yard under that big Douglas fir tree. Real honest-to-goodness grass, not the emerald moss that loves to take root during the winter.

So he tears out the moss. He aerates the soil. He fertilizes and he spreads a lush carpet of seed. Then he ropes off the area with pink and orange tape to warn away any fools who dare step on his lawn. So for months, as soon as the sun is warming and we all want to be outside, we are allowed to go outside and look at the pink-bordered lawn, but not actually to walk across it.

Keith's grass looks nice for a week. We get to mow it about once, and then it slowly starts dying as the moss takes over. Hey, it's green. Visually, I'm good with moss. Beats fluorescent pink tape in geometric shapes in the side yard.

I have a number of Sisyphus moments myself. Like trying to get the kids to like kale. Kale soup with beans and sausage, kale and garlic, kale chips . . . No go; but I keep rolling that deep green boulder up the same hill, and it rolls back down with the disappointed sounds of my children.

"Eewwww!"

It made me wonder: are we biologically wired for optimism? Turns out we are! Evidently, the way our frontal cortex communicates with regions deep in our brain gives us this sunny outlook. It may be why we dare get married, even. Statistics show that 40 percent of all marriages end in divorce; but, ask any newlywed and he or she will most likely tell you that it would never happen to them. That's a 0 percent likelihood. This is math. Can't argue with it. Ever try and argue with math? Our wiring makes us more optimistic than realistic.

It may be why we have children, why we bring new life into a complicated world.

It may be why I continue to try and get the kids to clean their rooms, make their beds, organize their projects, and get along with each other.

I am simply a victim of my frontal cortex.

It kind of takes the Sisyphean edge off things.

When Leo was born, Kai was two years old. We read all the articles about sibling rivalry and how the older sibling would eventually just want to toss the baby out or send it back. Kai loved Leo from the get-go. He adored him—he never wanted to send him back, he always wanted to hold him, he talked to him incessantly, he told him stories, he played with him. It was wonderful.

Keith and I congratulated each other on our outstanding parenting skills. All was well in the kingdom, until Leo got old enough to have his own opinions and ideas. Suddenly, the sibling rivalry thing emerged. Hello, Sisyphus.

To this day, we have almost daily conversations about cooperation, and family, and feelings, and love, and how hard it is sometimes to talk through things when you are mad but how much better that is than to lash out . . .

Daily.

It never fails: when one of the boys is in trouble for something, the other one immediately compliments my cooking, my hair, or clothing—anything in order to outshine the other. They polish their halos. Sometimes they glow with the effort of the polish, and I feel that I have a mini Eddie Haskell meets Shirley Temple in my house.

This halo polishing only serves to wrangle the ire of the other—the "bad" one—and the next thing you know they've set up the perfect ring for a rumble. Tempers flare, voices increase in pitch and volume, and I'm starting to wonder how my neighbors are enjoying the show—especially from me.

"Stop fighting and remember you *love* your brother."

"I do *not*."

"You do, too! And here's the thing, you are going to have each other for your *whole* lives. He's the only brother you are ever going to have. You'll need each other when you get older to talk about how frustrated you are with your parents. And then even later than that, when you compare stories of your childhood, you will have a built-in audience that TOTALLY understands because he had the same parents. It's *good*."

"It is not. Kai is *mean*."

"I'm mean? *Leo's* mean!"

"I am NOT mean. You are."

"No, YOU ARE."

"No, you!"

"You."

"Uh-uh."

"Uh-huh!"

"Boys. Boys. BOYS! STOP FIGHTING! YOU LOVE EACH OTHER! NOW BE QUIET!"

Mommy of the year.

I had to find a way to be the grown-up, so I decided to toss a little science into the mix.

"OK, guys, sit down and listen to me. I am going to explain why you are having these impulses to fight. It's your lizard brain."

Both boys were silent.

They looked at each other, and their eyes widened. I thought they would think this was super cool, since they both had an affection for lizards.

They looked back at me and burst into tears.

"Wait! What's wrong?"

"Mommy, that was really the *meanest* ever!"

"Yeah! MEAN MOM! We do not have lizard brains!"

Leo ran down the hall, yelling "DAAAADDDY! Mommy called us lizard brains!" Kai on his heels. Both in tears.

Backfire. But at least they were united.

I heard Keith's soothing voice assuring them, "There must be a misunderstanding because Mommy isn't known to call you names. Plus I don't think she thinks you have lizard brains."

I grabbed a book with beautiful pictures of the brain—MRI cross sections, drawings, schematics. I got it for Christmas when I was in college, and I can't tell you how often I gaze at the pages and marvel. I hooked the spine with my finger and joined my family down the hall.

"They *do* have lizard brains."

"MOM!"

"Wait. We all do. Let me show you."

I opened the book and showed them the curlicued cortex. "This is the part of our brains where we form thoughts and language and words and memories. It's soft, like cold oatmeal."

"Ew, cool," said Kai.

"The folds and bumps are called gyri and sulci. We have them all over. Rat brains don't have these bumps and folds."

"Ha-ha! Jackson told me that *gyri* means 'diarrhea' in Japanese!"

Leo looked at him and collapsed in laughter.

"Can we get a rat, Mom? I hear they make great pets. They're super smart," pleaded Kai.

"Kai, they don't have folds in their brain, how smart can they be?" corrected Leo. "But *can* we get one, Mom?"

"No. No rodents, no reptiles, remember?"

"But Mom . . ."

"Look! Our brains are amazing. Squeezed into this gooey mass of bumps and folds are billions of nerve cells. Billions! That's such a huge number, it's really hard to even imagine."

"More than your book collection?"

"Way more."

"More than the blades of grass in the lawn?"

"Way more."

"How about the stars at night?"

"More."

"Wow."

"And these cells are like highways that chemicals and electricity travel along. When that happens you move, you think, you sneeze, you breathe, you laugh, see stuff, hear stuff, or smile. Everything."

"So why did you call us lizard brains?" Kai asked.

"Because we all have a part of our brains deep inside that is a lot like lizard brain. It sits at the base of the skull, at the top of the spine. It's our old brain. We've had it inside our bigger brains since way, way, way back in time when we were—well—lizards. It's important to us. In fact, we couldn't live without it. This part of our brain has only a few messages: eat, attack, run away, or mate."

"Ew! Mom!"

"Seriously, the lizard brain is all about survival. It isn't about thinking or writing poetry or making cupcakes. It's about surviving. And sometimes this part of the brain fires before we get a chance to control what it tells us."

"What?"

"When you get mad at your brother and pop him on the noggin or throw a Lego across the room, it's your lizard brain at work."

"So if we can't help it, why do you yell at us?"

"I *don't* yell! Well, OK, sometimes I do, and that's *my* lizard brain working."

"See? It isn't easy."

"You're right, it's not. But you can reroute the traffic. You can make a detour in your brain and stop yourself from doing things that hurt other people."

"Because I'm not really a lizard?" asked Kai.

"Right. We have a part of us that will always be lizard-like, but we have this bigger pile of oatmeal here that can help us do the right thing. 'Cause you guys know that hitting and yelling and throwing things aren't the right thing to do, right?"

"Maybe."

"OK, so the next time your brother does something to annoy you and you feel like you're going to explode, stop. Take a deep breath. Count to ten, and you *will* calm down."

"How do you know?"

"It's science. When something bugs you, that triggers your brain to respond. In our brains, the lizard part of the brain is going cuckoo-crazy. It happens lightning fast. The message your lizard brain is sending is 'Hit your brother!' or 'Scream!' or 'Throw that book across the room!'

"The bad news is that the lizard brain doesn't usually have *great* ideas unless you're running from danger or trying to survive something. The good thing is that your heart starts pumping and the blood starts flowing to all parts of your brain—including this front part. Right here, over your left eye. This part of your brain helps you think about things. It knows right from wrong. It's the part that will tell your lizard brain that hitting your brother isn't right.

"The problem is that the lizard brain is a little faster, so you need to give this front part a little time to catch up. You have to help it along."

"How?"

"Take a deep breath, and the oxygen feeds your body. It relaxes. Then if you count, you force the electricity and chemicals down a detour through the front part of your brain. It doesn't go to Lizard Central. Then you can maybe even use words to say why you are frustrated. That reroutes the chemicals and electricity over here to the language center. Before you know it, you don't feel like clobbering your brother anymore. Lizard brain settles down."

"What if I *want* to clobber Leo?"

"I would clobber *you* back!" Leo said, and whacked Kai on the back.

Kai turned and poked him in the stomach and yelled, "Leo, I hate you!"

The two of them tussled until Keith and I pulled them apart.

"Take a deep breath!"

They did.

"Count to ten."

They did.

"Kai, say why you are frustrated with Leo."

"Because he hit me for no reason."

"I had a reason, Kai."

"OK Leo, why did you hit Kai?"

"Because he said he wanted to hit me. I hate that. I hate him."

"I hate you, too!"

"WAIT! Breathe!"

They did.

"You don't really hate Leo, do you?"

"No."

"And Leo, you don't really hate Kai, right?"

"I don't hate him."

"It was your lizard brain at work! Did you feel how fast it happened?"

"Yeah."

"And do you see how calm you are now?"

"I *guess*."

"And you *love* each other. You are brothers. Each of you is the *only* brother you are ever going to have . . . and you have to be aware of your lizard brains and try not to let them control you."

"Mom."

"Yes, Love?"

"Can we get a lizard?" asked Leo.

"Pleeeease, Mom?" added Kai.

"You each have one already—inside. Take care of it and keep it calm."

I looked at Keith. He smiled at me.

"Nice one, Mama."

"Thanks, Honey."

"Hey guys. I have an idea. We're going to start a project."

"OK, have fun." Keith said. "I'm going outside to get rid of that moss and plant some grass. No one step inside the lines!"

"What project, Mom?"

"We're going to make a huge garden lizard out of concrete, and then we're going to mosaic it and put it where we can all see it every day, to remind us."

The lizard project is still ongoing. It may never be finished. It sits just beyond the tape perimeter in the yard around Keith's grass. We dug the shape out in the old sandbox and put concrete in. Then flipped it. It's huge. It looms. We have mosaicked maybe half of it with old dishes that we broke or found at yard sales. It's impressive.

We have a name for him. We call him Sisyphus. He is a rock-solid example for all of us. A fixture in our lives to remind us again and again that it takes endless optimism (and effort, not to mention frontal cortex) to even think we can override our lizard brains. He sits unfinished and beckoning. And forever we will happily imagine finishing him, though we kind of like him just the way he is.

GARDEN LIZARD MOSAIC

We are eternally making our garden lizard mosaic, but this sand casting allows you to make anything you like. Maybe a turtle? Maybe a snake?

FOR THE SAND-CASTED LIZARD
WHAT YOU NEED

- Bucket
- Quikrete (see below)
- Water
- Stirring stick (paint stirrers work well)
- Sand in a sandbox or bin
- Rubber gloves
- Safety goggles

WHAT'S THE DIFFERENCE BETWEEN CEMENT AND CONCRETE?

To tell you the truth I never even thought about it until I decided to make this project. Cement, concrete, you say tomato . . . But they are, in fact, different.

Cement is an ingredient in concrete. It's made of limestone, sand, and clay. Technically speaking, the important chemicals here are calcium, silicon, aluminum, and iron. It's like a glue that holds together the stuff in concrete.

Concrete is a mixture of cement, water, and sand or small pebbles. It's tougher and stronger. Personally, I use Quikrete brand fast-setting concrete. It's cheap, easy to find in hardware stores, and works well.

It comes as a powder that you mix with water, and eventually it dries and hardens into a rocklike substance.

Fun stuff!

WHAT YOU DO

1. Prepare the sand. The sand needs to be moist to hold the shapes you dig out, so moisten it with water if it hasn't rained recently.
2. Make a mold of your creature. Using a stick or a spoon or hands, scoop out your creature. Now remember, this is the reverse of what you want. So when you dig the shape, the back will be the farthest point down in the sand. After it hardens, it will be flipped around. Make sure there aren't any crumbly areas in the sand. Whatever marks are there will show up in the concrete.
3. Mix the concrete according to the package directions. Scoop the powdered concrete into the bucket, and slowly add the water. You might want to wear a dust mask, goggles, and gloves.
4. Quick! Pour the concrete! Gently pour the concrete into your shape. Smooth out the back with a paint-stirring stick or something flat. If it's hot and sunny out, you'll need to cover the concrete lightly with plastic wrap so it doesn't dry too quickly and crack.
5. Wait for it to dry. Be patient—you may have to wait overnight. When the concrete has set up, you will know because it will be hard to the touch.
6. Dig it! Using your hands, carefully scoop the sand from around the shape. Wiggle it out, flip it over, and let it sit for 1 to 2 hours to completely dry out.
7. Clean it off. Use a paintbrush to get rid of all the extra sand you can.

FOR THE MOSAIC
WHAT YOU NEED

- Items to use as tiles (such as broken pieces of dishes, tiles, or glass; bottle caps; sea glass; marbles; pebbles; and toys)
- Thin set adhesive (you can find this at the hardware store)
- Putty knife
- Grout (this also can be found at the hardware store, and you can get it in a number of different colors; make sure you get the kind of grout made for outdoor use)
- Sponge
- Rubber gloves
- Bucket for mixing the grout
- Bucket for clean water

WHAT YOU DO

1. Make your tiles. We collected plates that we'd broken and gathered old tiles and smashed them for pieces, but you can use anything from bottle caps to sea glass to toys.
2. Prepare the surface. Use a paintbrush to get rid of all the sand you can.
3. Stick it. Spread the adhesive on a small section of the concrete animal. Spread it like cream cheese on a bagel.
4. Place tiles and pieces into the adhesive. Create the pattern you want. You can fly by the seat of your pants like I do, or you can organize it and even make a mock-up on paper. When you get all your pieces glued down, wait overnight for the glue to dry.
5. Apply the grout. Once the adhesive is dry, you want to mix your grout according to the instructions on the package. Wearing rubber gloves, smear the grout all over the piece, filling in the cracks between the pieces. The whole piece should look covered with grout when you are done. Using a damp sponge, wipe the entire piece to get rid of all the excess grout from the surface of the mosaic.
6. Let it dry.

6

OK, PLAY WITH THE FIRE

"Can we have s'mores tonight, Mama?"

Both Kai and Leo stand before me, shoulder to shoulder, with bright, open, pleading eyes. It's summer. The air is warm. The light is pink and low.

We're camping in the Olympic National Park. The water twinkles in the distance with the last of the evening light. We've spent the day wading in tide pools and being dazzled by sea stars the size of our heads in oranges, purples, and crimsons. We've been tousled by salt spray and sun.

I love camping. I really do. Time to reconnect with the environment, fantasize about what it might have been like to be living off the land thousands of years ago (except with a great tent, a cozy sleeping bag, and fleece and down). Food tastes better. Stories and games are fun. So many ways to give the kids perspective. As beings on the planet, we're pretty small, when you get right down to it. Getting out in the wilderness helps you see it.

Even if we're met with the inevitable whining because of no TV or screens during a camping trip, it is soon overthrown by the sense of adventure. I love it so much I even wrote a book about it: *Camp Out!* This comes back and bites me, though. Whenever I ask Keith to weigh in on anything that happens when we're camping, his favorite response is, "Don't ask me; *you* wrote the book."

When we go camping, I am outnumbered in the gender department three to one. My own experience camping taps into my cavewoman brain. I enjoy gathering berries, looking at leaf shapes, settling into camp, pitching the tent, telling stories, and making things.

Kai, Leo, and Keith utilize their caveman brains by starting the fire and being absolutely and totally mesmerized by that fire—finding more exciting ways to set it ablaze, with sticks, leaves, marshmallows.

"Can we *make a fire* and then can we make s'mores? Please Mama, please, Mama, pleeeeeeease?"

I am no dummy. It is not the sticky-sweet melty treat they're after. It's *fire* they desire. They want to light it, watch it, stick things into it, and watch them burn. And why not? Fire is one of the things that separate humans from the rest of the animals. It's sheer power. Human beings are the only creatures on the planet that create and use fire for their own purposes. Power, amazement, and danger sometimes go hand in hand. The trick is knowing when to let the kids hold a little of that danger in their own hands.

It's easy to imagine Smokey the Bear crying at the devastation that we singularly inflict on the planet with one simple strike of a match. Not to mention the burnt appendages and sizzled skin of my two beautiful boys. I clenched. I fretted. I stalled. While I sent the boys off with Keith to get some fresh water, I worried about boys and fire and destruction and pain and gazed at the plastic bag of marshmallows. I spotted the warning right away.

WARNING: EAT ONE AT A TIME. FOR CHILDREN UNDER SIX, CUT MARSHMALLOWS INTO BITE-SIZE PIECES. CHILDREN SHOULD ALWAYS BE SEATED AND SUPERVISED WHEN EATING.

What have we become? As parents, we all want to protect our babies in ways even better than our own parents did; but are we making a huge mistake? If we round every corner and eliminate every danger from their lives, when they inevitably come into contact with something dangerous, they'll never know how to act, and they'll surely do damage.

We can't do everything for them. We need them to learn, discover, create, fail, try again, and interact with the world.

When my friends were having kids, I was the happy "auntie" that came to visit. I was nowhere near ready to do that yet; but I watched. I remember one little girl had it all. She had a plastic kitchen I envied, a beauty parlor, and every single plastic version of any kind of pretend toy there was. It's great to teach children to pretend. They learn so much that way. They learn about the world. It made sense.

Then I visited another friend who did not offer the world of plastic toys to her kid. As a result, this kid made toys from what she found. She had seen an electrician come in to the house the day before, and crafted a tool belt out of a toilet paper roll and some tape. I'm sure she would have had fun pretending with a real plastic version of an electrician's tool belt; but, left to her own devices, she created something, solved the problem, and developed an extended sense of self through the tools and through the idea that she could do anything to make those tools appear. That was a gift. The mom was apologetic and embarrassed because her kid was playing with trash, but I loved it. It was a pivotal moment for me as a one-day parent. Give the time to the kids to create their own tools. To come to their own mastery. There should be space and permission to push their own boundaries.

I didn't want to be the parent that minced marshmallows into tiny pieces and observed my kid chewing every morsel. I didn't want to be the mom that hovered. I carried a pail of water with me wherever I went in our campsite. I helicoptered. Until I realized there might be a little science to all this. A little science and a whole lot of freedom.

Fire is a force of nature, to be sure. Fire is mysterious, magical, scary, delightful, friendly, and fierce all together. Maybe that mystery is only revealed—as many things are—to those who play with it. Those who look and experience it. Those who respect and learn how to control it. Seems to me that the fire is a lab.

"You guys are going to start the fire tonight, and yes, we can have s'mores."

"YES!" they both shrieked. They darted over to Keith, who was looking at me with surprise.

"Hey, I wrote the book!"

"Dad, Mom said we could light the fire, so where is the lighter fluid?" Kai asked.

"Hang on, fire boy!" I clarified. "You will light the fire from scratch."

"Yeah, I know from scratch, like Daddy does with that liquid in the white bottle."

I was horrified.

"No," I said. "We're going to build a fire from scratch."

"You mean like rub two sticks together, like the Flintstones?"

"Well, no—maybe someday we'll try that. We'll use a match, but here's the challenge. We only use *one* match. We pretend we need to survive, and we only have one match to do it. You ready? The fate of our s'mores lies with you tonight."

Kai and Leo looked at each other and grinned.

"OK, so what do we do?" Kai asked.

"What is fire?" I asked back.

"Hot," Leo said.

"Duh, Leo, of course it's hot—how else will it burn the marshmallows?" Kai said. And then he asked, "It's not alive, is it, Mom?"

"Technically it's not alive like you and I are, but I think it's a smart idea to maybe think of it as alive in some way. It has power. You have to feed it and take care of it. It can even seem angry sometimes and get out of control and destroy stuff and kill things."

"I don't want to light a fire, Mom," said Leo, suddenly sheepish.

"It's OK, Love. If you treat it right and respect it, the fire will be your marshmallow-searing pal. First things first. We need fire food. What does it eat?"

"Wood!"

"Yes!"

"Sticks!"

"Yes!"

"Dried leaves!"

"Yes!"

"Marshmallows!"

"Not at first, Leo, but soon."

They were off gathering. This satisfied the cavewoman mama in me. I watched them forage near the campsite. I grinned smugly at Keith, who was watching me watch them.

"OK, Ms. Smarty-pants. What is fire? I mean, really, can you explain it to me?"

"It's hot. How else would it burn the marshmallows?"

"Well, good luck, Miss One Match. I don't even have the starter fluid."

We spent a good hour gathering dried grasses, leaves, small twigs, bigger twigs, and sticks. We had brought our own firewood. We arranged the materials in a kind of small pile with bigger sticks and firewood leaning in to a point, like a tepee.

"Why a tepee, Mom?"

"Well, when it comes to making and feeding a fire it's all about the dried stuff to burn, but it's also all about the air. It's a triangle. You need air, fuel like sticks and dried grasses, and heat."

We were ready. Kai struck the match and ignited the dried grasses. Leo cheered. The two boys wriggled with expectation. Keith leaned over and watched.

"Needs air," he said, and blew gently. It took! The twigs were engulfed and finally the small sticks lit up. The boys carefully put small twigs on until the tepee of twigs caught.

"Now add a small piece of firewood."

Kai gently placed a piece of wood on the fire. It was a good fire.

"FIRE!" Leo shrieked and danced around it, whooping. "My turn to put a piece of wood on it!"

He gently placed a small log. They had risen to the challenge; for hours, they cared for their fire as if it were alive.

That night as everyone slept, my hair still smelling of campfire and chocolate, I grabbed my phone, and even though I had put the kibosh on screens, I couldn't resist doing a little research on what the heck fire really was.

It starts on a very small level. Fire happens when molecules rearrange their atoms.

What does that mean?

When iron rusts, oxygen atoms in the air mingle with the iron atoms and change them. It happens pretty slowly, and what results is rust. There is some heat along the way, but not a lot. So, with a flame, oxygen mingles with the molecules and the reaction happens so fast that the heat can't get out of its own way, and fire results.

I wasn't sure if I really understood it, but that's OK. What I did understand is that fire is a force. It gives off heat and light. It pulls people in. Controlling it is one thing that makes us human. We're drawn to it. We create myths around it. We tell stories around it and we simply watch and wonder.

The next morning, we weren't done with fire. Are we ever done with fire? As we sipped our assorted hot beverages around the campfire, Kai piped up.

"Mom, we made that fire yesterday on our own."

"Yeah, we did."

"Except how does that match work?"

"Let's look."

I pulled out a match. "The red part is chemicals that light up when you rub them hard and fast, and the wood is the fuel." I showed them.

"Yeah, but people made that match, right? So we didn't actually make that fire on our own."

"Yeah, we cheated," added Leo.

"Can we do it on our own?" Kai asked.

"I guess so . . ." I spotted Kai's backpack with his notebook, crayons, and a magnifying glass.

"Grab your magnifying glasses, get some dried grasses, and follow me."

We went to a sunny spot, made a ring of stones with the grass in the middle. I aimed the glass so that the sun shone through and made a small circle of light on the grass.

"You guys have the power to change sunlight into fire with this magnifying glass."

"How?"

"You're taking the light from the sun, which has energy, and you're kind of smushing it together and focusing the rays in one section. That's a lot of heat. Hold it steady and see what happens to your dried grass."

It wasn't done in an instant. It took several stops and starts; but eventually, there was smoke, and then there was fire.

"Mommy, is this how cavemen did it?"

"Well, they didn't have magnifying glasses. I suspect that maybe way long, long, long ago, there might have been a natural fire made by lightning, and man trapped a bit of it on the end of a stick. Then nursed it and kept that flame going.

"They learned it was hot, saw that it gave off light, learned to cook meat with it, and probably because it was so precious, they may have honored it with stories and rituals."

"Like we did last night?"

"Like we do when we gather and hang out together and tell stories and laugh. In a way, it's like we're connecting with cavemen."

"I like camping."

"Me too."

"I miss TV and stuff, but I like going back to olden days in my mind. Did they have marshmallows back then?"

"Probably not."

"Well, I'm glad I only go back there in my head."

"Can we have s'mores tonight? Pleeeeeeease!"

"If you make the fire, I'll find the marshmallows."

MAKE A FIRE

You can safely make a fire by using the mysterious and scientific combination of intake (wood for burning), combustion (flame), and exhaust (smoke).

What You Need

- A grown-up
- A fire pit
- Matches
- A few big handfuls of dried grasses, pine needles, or pine cones
- A few big handfuls of dry tiny twigs
- A few big handfuls of pencil-size twigs
- A few big handfuls of thumb-thickness twigs about 1 foot long
- A few armloads of wrist-thickness logs about 1 foot long

- A few armloads of leg-thickness logs up to 2 feet long
- A bucket of water (just in case)

What You Do

1. Make a ball of dried grass or pine needles. Put it in the center of the fire pit.
2. Next, place a handful of tiny twigs on top.
3. Take your pencil-size twigs, and make a tepee around the ball of grass. Make sure to leave a small opening for a match.
4. Make a larger tepee around the small teepee with the thumb-size twigs. Leave about a finger's-width space between the sticks.
5. Take the wrist-size logs and make a tepee around the twig tepee.
6. Strike a match, and touch the flame to the ball of grass or needles within the tepees. Blow gently to ignite the flame.
7. Let the tepees catch fire and burn. Practice patience and endurance—you'll need to nurse the fire, adding more twigs, blowing on it, making sure it doesn't topple—until you're certain it's OK on its own.
8. Carefully add bigger logs to the fire by gently placing them in a tepee shape around the flame. As the logs burn and then start to turn to glowing embers, you may want to add more logs to keep the fire burning.
9. Keep the bucket of water handy in case you need to douse the fire in a hurry. When the fire dies naturally, make sure it's out all the way by dousing it with water.

Everyone knows how to make the traditional s'mores with a slab of chocolate and a hot marshmallow between two graham crackers. But there's no need to limit yourself. Here are some ideas to get you started.

- Mint-flavored chocolate or a peanut butter cup and a roasted marshmallow between graham crackers
- Sliced bananas and a roasted marshmallow between coconut cookies

- Peanut butter, jelly, and a roasted marshmallow between graham crackers
- Apple slices, peanut butter, chocolate, and a roasted marshmallow between graham crackers
- Strawberry slices and a roasted marshmallow between shortbread cookies
- Raspberry jam, dark chocolate, and a roasted marshmallow between shortbread cookies
- Pineapple slices and a roasted marshmallow between coconut cookies
- Orange marmalade, dark chocolate, and a roasted marshmallow between vanilla wafers
- Pear slices, cinnamon chips, and a roasted marshmallow between graham crackers

7

PENNIES IN THE LEMONS

I'M NOT SURE I could have thrived as a pioneer. I'm not sure I would have been a successful Pilgrim. I don't think I would have enjoyed the Dark Ages. I'm pretty sure my kids wouldn't love it, either. Though we do try, when the situation arises. We do try.

Our first year on the island was wonderful—discovering new paths through the forests, finding new and interesting plants waking up in the spring, delighting in birds that visited in the summer, and thrilling to the fall colors.

The first winter brought cold, dark days. We had the lights on a lot. Had to! Even during the daytime, the lights were on. The sun doesn't come up around here in the winter until about 8:00. That's three hours past when our day starts. I also made the place cheery with trails of white twinkle lights draped in the fichus tree and in the corner by my favorite chair on a twisty branch. It was cozy. It was charming.

Our electricity bill was a stunner the first year.

Then the winter winds began to blow. We hunkered down in our cozy nest. I taught the boys how to light candles and respect the flame. The wind blew for days. The trees whipped and danced dangerously in the storm. The Douglas fir trees that dotted our property were bowing impossibly low. These are big trees. If one snapped and landed on the house, we'd be smushed.

Keith had a business meeting out of town, and on the first night, the wind was so bad that the local weather guys were warning people to sleep in the northwest corners of the first floor of their houses. Yikes! Where was the northwest corner of our house? The kitchen? Where was my compass?

I pitched the tent in the middle of the kitchen and blew up mattresses, and we went "camping." The boys had fun and fell asleep quickly. It was a long night for me. I stayed up listening to the house creak and the trees outside hiss and bend. Our dog, Kona, was petrified. She spent the night on top of me, quivering. The power flashed in and out, and every single appliance beeped when it went off and again when it went on. Things were beeping all night. My mattress had a slow leak, and by morning I was flat on the floor with a quivering dog and a back spasm.

But the power was back. The sun even made a show, and the wind had ended. We weathered the storm; however, that was just the beginning.

The year Kai was five and Leo was three was a big one. After months of dousing rain and spongy ground, the wind kicked in and threatened the shallow-rooted Douglas firs again. This time the wind was relentless. For a week, the wind blew. Our patio umbrella set sail and ended up down the street, impaled into the neighbor's front lawn. It looked very inviting.

The kids were old enough to feel scared about the force of the wind. I certainly was old enough to feel scared about the force of the wind.

"Mom, why is the wind so mad?" asked Kai.

"Is the wind mad at us?" Leo jumped in.

"The wind seems mad, doesn't it, because it's making so much noise and knocking things over; but it's not. It's just huge and powerful and cool."

"I'm scared," Leo said. He was. So was I.

Keith, a dyed-in-the-wool California guy, rolled with every weather scare with grace. Nothing fazed him.

"It's no big deal, guys," he'd say, and go about his business. He never panicked. I keep hoping that will rub off on me; but I decided to lean on science to diffuse the fear and turn it into respect.

"What is wind, and where does it come from?

"Here's the thing. The weather is everything that happens out there, right? It's the sun and the rain and the clouds and the wind. And it's all connected. We live under an ocean of air. There's a mile-high blanket of air all around the planet and it pushes down and in on us all the time. It's fine—because it's what we know.

"Sometimes that blanket kind of sloshes around. The sloshing makes the air move faster or slower, or go higher or sink lower. Those changes are the wind. It can be light and breezy, or really powerful," I told them.

"That's cool," Kai said.

"It is. So now that we know about it, we just have to be smart about how we build things and keep things so the wind won't mess up our stuff. It's not the wind. It's our responsibility to take care of things."

It worked. Turning the fear to fascination made the boys look out the window and want to go outside and explore. We tied old rags to sticks and stuck them in the ground. We watched how they moved in the wind. All together, or all over the place. Keith even made a whirl-igig wind catcher with old sippy cups on a wheel stuck to a piece of pipe. He put it in the garden.

"Now we can look at the sippy cups and see how fast the wind is blowing," he said.

I was, once more, joyfully reminded of why I had married this man.

The wind died down. We breathed a sigh of relief.

Then it snowed. A beautiful, wet, heavy snow that covered everything in icing. It was delicious—until it bent trees and snapped branches, and the branches bent and snapped the power lines.

The power went out.

Our house became a boot camp for electricity addicts. We played games by candlelight and taught the boys how to make a fire. We grilled everything outside. We roasted hot dogs and marshmallows and toast on sticks over the fire pit. We did everything over the fire—even coffee and pancakes.

"We're camping!" We'd cheer. It was fun.

The romantic notion of living with candles and firelight was really fun the first day. That night was cold, but we unfurled our down bags in front of the fire. Keith and I took turns stoking the fire so it wouldn't go out while we slept.

The second day was still fun. Kind of. We had s'mores for breakfast. We read about electricity and talked about the miracles it affords us. We imagined how it was to live in the olden days and pictured ourselves as pioneers or Indians.

I told the boys real tales of polar bears. I used to be a wildlife guide at the Central Park Zoo, and Gus, the famous pacing polar bear, and I had a history. I told them polar bears were really black.

"Nu-uh!"

"Uh huh!"

"Mom, they're white!"

"Nope. They just look white. There's more to a polar bear than meets the eye. Their hair is clear and hollow, and it bounces the sunlight back as white. The skin of a polar bear is jet black."

"I never see black polar bears."

"And you won't, unless it's been shaved."

"Why are they black?"

"I'll show you."

We put out black construction paper and white construction paper. On each we put a glass of snow. We put them both in the sun and checked it periodically to see which one melted faster. The black one did.

"Black absorbs the heat. That's why the car feels so hot on a sunny day. The black seats soak up all the heat from the sun. So it's good for polar bears, because the sun goes into their clear hair and right down into the black skin, warming up the bear."

"Hmm."

OK, that took up maybe an hour or so of day. More puzzles. More games. More candlelight. Still no power.

On Day Three we got together with friends. We commiserated. We put on shows, had flashlight fun, played charades. We made bread on a stick and even tried making pizza on a stick. It dripped a lot, but it was tasty. Still fun.

Day Four was harder. We made a pizza-box solar oven, and it took all afternoon to make nachos.

Day Five was a challenge. The newness of pioneer living was wearing thin on the boys. They were chilly, dirty, and lacking in enthusiasm.

Or was that me?

I decided to embrace the notion of wanting the power back. We talked about Ben Franklin and how when he was alive people didn't have electricity. "They had only candles and fire; but he was curious about some scary things—things like lightning. He thought it was electricity. Not many people agreed. So he did some experiments with a kite and a key in a thunderstorm. He was lucky he didn't get zapped; but we were lucky, too, because now all the electric appliances and lights happened because of his experiments."

We made lists of the things that need electricity.

The days were long. We even talked about circuits and made a few out of marshmallows and sticks.

Day Six. Still no power, and Mama was losing her steam.

Leo surprised me. "Mom? Can we do more electric stuff?"

Maybe this wave of no power was a gift.

"Did you know you can make a battery out of a lemon and some pennies, nails, and some copper wire?"

"Let's do it!" they hollered. I was delighted by their zeal. Plus, I knew we could stretch this activity out all day.

We had some lemons; Keith gathered the galvanized nails and copper wire and an LED bulb; the kids grabbed pennies from their banks and spent hours sorting them. Pennies were only copper before 1982. This set the boys off on a sorting spree.

Eventually we connected the wire to the nail and the pennies and stuck them into the lemons and attached the other ends to the LED bulb and ZING! We had light! It was magical.

It was a tiny light, but it was a wonderful feeling nevertheless. We cheered! We did a little jig. That night, as we tucked the boys into their bags in the living room by the fire, we talked about electricity and power and connection and circuits.

The next morning, the kids were already up when we got up. They had been tinkering on their own with different projects. Drawing, making stuff out of play dough, and playing with the circuit.

Wired together was every lemon, potato, turnip, baby carrot, and apple we had. When we got to them, they were trying to figure out how to hook the wires up to the TV.

I realized where the zeal for learning about power was headed. They respected the olden days but were tired of them. They were craving *Sponge Bob.*

I was craving *Sponge Bob.*

It was Day Seven of the power outage, with no relief in sight. Keith and I looked at each other. We had made the connection between us. Our circuit was complete. The light bulbs flashed on. We packed up and went to Seattle—to a hotel.

It was heaven. The kids watched *Sponge Bob.* I took a shower. We had room service, and we all celebrated the magic of electricity and the fact that we live in the twenty-first century.

When a big change happens to your routine and your situation, ideally you want to teach your kids to meet the challenges with creativity, ingenuity, and a welcoming sense of adventure. It's life, right? When things change, we need to change with them. We need to roll with it. Why not try to instill a sense of fun (and even science) in the midst of it?

Then again, you have to recognize when enough is enough.

LEMON BATTERY-POWERED CLOCK

Use a couple of lemons and a few things like wires and nails to power a small, low-voltage digital clock. One AA battery has about 1.5 volts of energy, and two lemons can produce about 1.5 volts as well. Pucker up and power up!

WHAT YOU NEED

- 2 ripe lemons
- Low-voltage digital clock (use a clock that takes 1 AA battery or a 1.5-volt button cell battery)

- 2 copper pennies (Check the dates. You'll need pennies dated from before 1982. Before then pennies were made with 95 percent copper. After 1982, pennies have been made with 97.5 percent zinc with a thin copper coating. The old pennies work better.)
- Three 8-inch lengths of copper wire
- 2 galvanized (zinc-coated) nails
- Knife

What You Do

1. Roll your lemons on a hard surface. You want them kind of squishy and juicy inside, but you don't want to break the skin.
2. Take one copper wire, and wrap one end around and around a penny. Wrap the other end around a galvanized nail.
3. Take a second wire, and wrap one end around a penny. Leave the other end open.
4. Take the third wire, and wrap it around a galvanized nail and leave the other end open.
5. Use a knife to cut a small slit in the left side of each lemon—just big enough for a penny. Insert a penny into each lemon, pushing it all the way in.
6. Take the nail from the other end of the attached penny, and stick it in the right side of the other lemon. Place the nail with the empty end on the right side of the penny that is attached to the other nail.
7. Your lemons should be connected, and you should have one with a nail and a bare wire and the other with a penny attached to a bare wire.
8. Take the battery out of the clock. Attach the wires to the positive and negative terminals in the clock. If your clock doesn't work, try switching the wires.
9. The clock should be working!

WHAT'S GOING ON?

The power is in the zinc, not the lemon. It's all about the flow of electrons.

When the zinc-coated nail comes in contact with the lemon juice, two reactions take place. The lemon juice starts taking zinc atoms off the nail. Then the juice separates the electrons from the atom. The rest of the zinc atom is positively charged and hangs out in the lemon juice. The electrons leap from the zinc nail, through the wire, and into the copper. The copper wire pulls on the electrons. Then the negatively charged electrons enter back into the juice of the lemon and make their way back to the positively charged atoms near the zinc. The flow of electrons is called a *circuit*. It flows in one direction. This flow is called *electric current*. Because there is a complete circuit, the electrons flow. It creates a battery.

Put something in the path of the circuit—like a clock—and the clock can use the energy of the flow.

8

MOMENTS OF MAGNETISM

IT WAS LABOR DAY, the day before Kai was to start kindergarten, and Keith and I decided to have a few folks over for a BBQ and a movie for the kids out in the woods at our makeshift outdoor theater. Pretty early on, when everyone was mingling around having fun, grilling various things, I heard a blood-scorching scream from upstairs.

When I got to the room, I spotted Kai on all fours, crying.

"KAI! What happened?"

"We were playing kitty cats and I was pretending to eat kitty food and I swallowed a magnet."

The exact thing you never want to hear your kid say he swallowed. "How many?"

"Just one!" he sobbed.

"Are you sure?"

"I don't know!"

You read about kids who swallow two or more magnets who die instantly because they click together inside, blocking key digestive pathways. How much time did we have?

"Don't panic," was what I was trying to say to myself; but Kai could tell I was freaked out. He's an astute kid. Plus, I was yelling, "OHMY-GOD I AM FREAKING OUT!"

My good friend Amy, a nurse, told me to rush to the emergency room, which I did, leaving Keith on his own amid the Labor Day revelry.

En route to the hospital, I recovered my savvy.

"This could be fun, Kai!"

He was *not* buying that.

"I mean, they'll X-ray you and you can see what your insides look like. That's pretty interesting. Isn't it?

"What's an X-ray?"

"Oh, it's fascinating! They shoot a kind of light through your body—it doesn't hurt—and then they catch the light after it bounces past things, so it's a way to see inside your body. You'll see bones and hard stuff. Isn't that cool? How many kids have pictures of their insides?"

"I guess."

"And you know what?"

"What?"

"Since you're a big kid now, going to big-kid school, I'll bet there's a science fair and maybe this could give you some ideas about what you might want to do for a project."

"Like X-rays?"

"Maybe. Let's see what inspires you."

We saw the X-rays and were relieved to see that he had only ingested one piece of magnetic "kitty food." Thank God for small "kitty" appetites.

The relief was short-lived when the doctor arrived with a copy of the X-ray for Kai to keep, a handful of tongue depressors, and a small, kidney-shaped plastic bowl.

"You're going to have to sort through the fecal material every day until the magnet is found," he said. He was even cheerful about it.

"What?" said Kai. "What is fecal material?"

"Poop."

"Really? You're kidding!" This was hilarious to him.

I knew what was ahead of us.

Ugh.

Days and days of sorting through poop. Was there a metaphor in this for us as parents?

On the way home, as we passed by bucolic scenes and pastures filled with goats, llamas, and cows, I had a thought. Cows!

Don't cows swallow magnets?

In seventh grade, I had been smitten with the James Herriot books and was desperate to become a veterinarian. I remember studying about cows and how farmers fed lozenge-shaped magnets to a cow so, when swallowed, a magnet would land in the first of four stomach chambers. The reason was because cows were not so discriminating about what they ate along with their grass. They often ate nails, barbed wire, or other sharp metal shards that may be lying amid the grasses. Toss a magnet in, and all the heavy metal sticks in the first stomach chamber, protecting the cows from being sliced up from the inside.

So if a cow swallowed a magnet, how did the cow vets know if the magnet was inside or not? And where? There had to be an easy way without X-raying Bessie every few weeks, right?

Suddenly I was pulled back to reality by the computerized voice of the GPS system, which I had forgotten to turn off. It gave me an epiphany. Maybe, just maybe, we could avoid searching through Kai's poop with sticks and track that magnet inside—with a compass! Since a compass needle points to the north pole of the planet, which is one huge magnet, couldn't it work on a tiny magnet?

We tried it as soon as we got home. We grabbed the nice compass—the one we take camping—and pointed it to Kai's belly. ZING! The needle whipped around and pointed directly to a spot in Kai's abdomen.

Every day we held up the compass to Kai's abdomen and moved it around until the needle moved and pointed definitively.

It was great! No wooden-stick poop diving. And we could actually see the path of the magnet as it took its winding intestinal journey. Which, I may add, took almost *three* weeks. I can't imagine twenty-one days of sifting with sticks.

Meanwhile, Kai and I looked at *Gray's Anatomy*. We checked out *The Anatomy Coloring Book* and looked online. We made drawings of intestines. We clocked the progress of that magnet with verve. We talked about digestion. We explored what poop was. We chatted about absorption, villi, colons, and finally, rectums.

It was a kindergartener's dream.

On the day the compass needle lazed around with no direction, we knew the culprit had been sprung and lay waiting for us in the bowl.

Keith grabbed a powerful magnet he had purchased for this event and stirred around the toilet until he found what we had all been looking for—for nearly a month. The thing was retrieved and dipped in bleach.

It was the centerpiece for Kai's first science fair project, entitled "I Swallowed a Magnet, So You Don't Have To."

We traced Kai's body on a big piece of cardboard and he filled in the intestines, eyes, mouth, and of course, the exit. He dictated countless facts he had learned—like "Your intestines stretch from here to Chip's house and back," and "If you have to swallow a magnet, only swallow one, because if you swallow two they will SNAP together and kill you instantly!" He has a flair for drama.

Then he took a magnet and taped it to a secret place behind the cardboard. He hung a compass on the hand and had me write out: *Find the magnet.*

It was the talk of the science fair—and not in the same way that the first grader who had "built" a working wind tunnel was talked about.

I felt a tap on my back. It was Kai. He was holding a ribbon. He also had a certificate. It was an award.

"MOM! I won!"

"Won what, Sweetie?"

He handed me the certificate especially designed for him. It said, "Congratulations, Kai, for Having the Stomach for Science!"

"Hurrah for you!"

He danced away into the crowd to show his teacher.

I was so proud of Kai. So proud that he learned how to take a tough situation and turn it into exploration and joy. I held my chin up, knowing I had been resourceful and truly utilized this as that sought-after "teachable moment."

I smiled as a group of women came up and exclaimed their admiration for the project. One woman's first grader was the one who had crafted a working wind tunnel out of Popsicle sticks and had secured a scale model of the Red Baron flying with scrawled writing describing what it was. His dad was a pilot. The other mom's kid had made a robotic T. rex, and it was walking around the gym on its own. They looked at each other, and then at me.

"Intriguing project. But it's a little dangerous, isn't it? To have Kai swallow a magnet for his science project?"

I looked at her in shock, as she smiled vacantly at me. Overachiever, yes; but I wasn't crazy!

"The things you have to do these days to be noticed for scholarships down the line!"

I had horrified her. I laughed, tapping her shoulder. She sort of smiled back to me.

"It's all about the crap factor!"

"What?" They clearly thought I was a lunatic and were inching away from me before turning to run.

"It was a magnet! We used a compass! We didn't want to deal with the Popsicle sticks . . . He was playing kitty cat . . . and you know how compasses are just like magnets and opposites attract, we just . . ."

They were gone.

"It was an accident," I said to no one. "We just made the best of it."

☰ 💡HEAVY METAL MEALS☰

Cows aren't the only creatures eating metal. Chances are you and your kids had a good dose of metal already this morning. Try this experiment and see for yourself. Check it out.

WHAT YOU NEED

- Iron-fortified cereal (find ones with 100 percent daily allowance of iron)
- Water
- Blender

- Big bowl
- Magnet

What You Do

1. Put 3 cups of iron-fortified cereal in the blender, and cover it with enough water to make a watery mush. Blend the mixture until it's really squishy and completely mush.
2. Place your magnet in the bottom of a bowl, and pour the mush over it. Swish it around and around.
3. Reach in and grab the magnet. Rinse it gently. Check out the fuzzy black coating—that's iron!

WHAT'S GOING ON?

Inside your innocent-looking bowl of iron-fortified breakfast cereal lurks a dusting of *real* metal iron. But don't worry, you need it. Everybody does. That's why manufacturers put it in there.

You've heard people talk. "You need your iron," "Eat spinach," and all that. It's true; you do need iron. Here's why. Your blood cells circulate all around your body bringing oxygen and other nutrients to every cell and taking waste away. But oxygen wouldn't have anything to hook on to if not for iron. No iron, no oxygen. So make sure you eat enough iron—but don't go around gnawing on nails.

DANCING PAPERCLIPS!

Check out this ordinary office-supply salsa dance. It's fun. It's easy. It's magnetic!

What You Need

- Metal paperclips
- Thread
- Tape
- Magnet
- Ruler

What You Do

1. Make a loop of tape and tape the magnet to one end of the ruler.
2. Tie one end of the thread to your paperclip. Tape the other end of thread to the table.
3. Wave the magnet over the paperclip and see if you can get it to jump up in the air. Don't let the magnet touch the clip. Watch it strain and hover!
4. Take it further. Make small paper fish, UFOs, bugs, or birds, and clip them to the paperclip. Hold the magnet over them and make them fly or dance or hover.

WHAT'S GOING ON?

The magnet is pulling on the metal of the clips, but because it doesn't actually make contact, the clips hover, pulling against the thread, trying to reach the magnet.

9

MOTHER OF THE YEAR

DID YOU KNOW HENRY WINKLER, the Fonz, writes books? He does. They're great. Plus, what is very cool is that he's dyslexic and has found elegant work-arounds and ways of expressing his creativity in spite of the hurdles put in his way.

I was getting ready to go see Henry Winkler read from his popular middle-grade fiction series over at the high school. I was excited to see him read, to learn about his process. I had asked Kai if he wanted to join me, thinking it would be a great way to get him more interested in reading. We could have great mommy-son bonding time. A lovely event to share and talk about later . . . HAH!

He had no idea who the Fonz was and was not impressed or the least bit interested. "A book reading, Mom? On a Saturday? No thanks!"

So Keith took him and Leo to practice lacrosse skills with the big boys who were trying to interest young guys in the game.

As I was about to leave, the phone rang. It was Keith. I could hear crying in the background.

Not good.

"Can you come get Kai? He fell and he doesn't want to play any-more."

"Is he OK?"

"I think so. He's just unhappy."

When I arrived he was dry-eyed. He had fallen on his arm, over his stick. I felt along the place and he winced. This did not surprise me. Like me, Kai is very in touch with his nerve endings. I made him flex his hands. Bend them up and down. Twist them. Do all sorts of exer-cises. Which he did, without pain. I was convinced we were fine. After all, I reasoned to myself, the muscles are attached to the bones, and if a bone was broken we would definitely know when a muscle pulled on it.

"I broke it, Mom!" He said.

"No you didn't, Honey. It would hurt a *lot* more. You're fine. Let's go see the Fonz!"

Tears. "Do I have to?"

"It will be fun! Plus, it's either that or stay here."

Soft and thoughtful moan. "OK."

The reading was fun. Kai even liked it after a good stint of pouting. Henry Winkler was delightful and spoke about dictating his novels to his partner: walking along single planks in the floor, like a tightrope, one foot in front of the other, as he pulled the stories from his head.

It was impressive and inspiring, but also sad in a way, as his parents and teachers treated him so badly in his youth. Nothing was known of dyslexia in that day and age, so he was dismissed. Poor guy. I would *never* do such a thing to *my* kid!

Never.

We bought the books and went home.

Later in the day, we went to the pool. The kids had a blast. Kai's arm was fine. That week he played baseball and swam and played; but strangely, when I asked him to make his bed he held his arm to his side like a broken wing and winced, saying he couldn't possibly make his bed because his arm was broken.

Right.

This went on for about four days, and then we had friends over. The kids were playing. Kai had been pretty grumpy, but I chalked it up to this or that, like needing food or sleep, or the other various variables that can be blamed—the moon, Mars in retrograde, you know.

Then one of the girls ran up, saying, "Kai is chasing me with an ax saying he's going to chop me up. He's freaking me out!"

"Oooooh, hey," I assured the wide-eyed mom with an unconvincing smile. "*That's* not like him!"

It really *wasn't* like him to attempt murder, but this was awkward. I found the cranky thing and asked what the problem was.

"I have a broken arm!" he wailed. "It hurts!"

"OK, but an ax? Come on! Plus you played baseball and swam . . . I don't think your arm is broken."

"The ax is PLASTIC! Besides, I *know* my arm is broken. MOM, WHY WON'T YOU BELIEVE ME?"

"Yeah, when it works for you. OK, big guy, if it's broken then I can call the doctor and I am sure there's a shot—a painful one—that he can give you for the pain."

HA! Take that!

"OK," he said.

What? The threat of a painful shot on top of seeing the doctor did nothing to dissuade? This may be a problem.

We went in.

The doctor checked him. I told the story, with appropriate eye rolls and smirks. "It hurts him when he makes his bed but not when he swims or plays baseball . . ."

"Well," she said gently. "I think it may be broken."

I know I looked shocked.

"Mom! I TOLD you!"

Now I am sure I looked horrified.

We had it X-rayed and then we went back into the doctor's office, where she came in with a basket of plaster and an assistant. "It's broken," she said, showing us the hairline fracture on the film.

Kai stood up with both arms in the air, emitting one enthusiastic pump and a long hissing "YESSSS!" He had won the arm-in-a-cast told-you-so-Mom lottery.

I was as bad as the Fonz's parents and teachers. I had dismissed my son! I cried as my son did the dance of victory.

"Why are you crying, Mommy?"

"It hurts, Honey."

I turned to the doctor. "Wouldn't it have really hurt more? Wouldn't a break be unmistakable?"

I was searching for validation.

"Sometimes these hairline fractures are so small they don't cause a lot of swelling or pain unless a specific movement makes the fracture bigger. Then it hurts more."

"So swimming and baseball didn't hit the pain place," I said.

"But Mom, I told you when I made my bed it really hurt! It was the pulling up of the covers."

The doctor turned to me and shrugged. "I guess it hurt to make the bed."

Again Kai pumped his fists in the air. "Ha-HA! I told you, Mom."

The doctor put a red cast on Kai's arm. He admired it and held it aloft as we exited the doctor's office.

"Want ice cream, Bub?"

"Yeah, sure."

"Good. It's good medicine."

"Mom, don't get me wrong. I love ice cream, but what does it have to do with my arm?"

"Well, ice cream is loaded with calcium and *you* need that, and it can come loaded with chocolate and *I* need that."

"Why calcium?" Kai held his cone in his right hand and licked happily away at it while making sure the red cast was visible to all who passed.

"Well, our bones are made up of a bunch of hard and soft stuff. They have to be both strong and flexible. They hold us up. They are anchors for our muscles and they protect us. They also have to be lightweight or it would be really hard to move. So bones are hard on the outside and full of stuff in the middle."

"Huh?"

"Yup. Picture a corn dog."

"Mom. I'm eating ice cream!"

"Bear with me. Picture a corn dog. If you take a bite you can see what's inside. It's like a bone. You have an outer crust. It's hard.

Crunchy. Then you have this layer of cornbread. It's flexible and it protects the hot dog within. The hot dog within is like the bone marrow. Bone marrow is like red jelly. Its job is to make red blood cells."

"OK."

"OK, so if you try and break a corn dog it bends first, right?"

"Yeah."

"And when it breaks the hard crust breaks first, right?

"Yeah, but . . ."

"That's just like your bone. When you fell on your lacrosse stick the stick pushed on the bone and it broke your corn dog. It didn't smash it or break it all the way through, but it put a dent in your corn dog's crust."

"OK, Mom. Corn-dog bone. But what's it got to do with ice cream?"

"Ice cream is loaded with calcium. This makes bones strong and hard."

"Does it make the crack disappear?"

"Yeah, in time. You were lucky it was only a crack. Sometimes bones break and the ends of the broken places are far apart. They have to be fitted back together like a jigsaw puzzle."

"That would hurt."

"It hurts just thinking about it, doesn't it?"

"Ow."

"But lucky for us, our bodies are miraculous and our bones kind of fix themselves."

"But how?"

"When bones are broken the first thing that happens is that broken blood vessels make a clot. The clot is the first part of the bridge that fixes the bone. After that, cells called fibroblasts come to the scene and multiply and squirt out this material that hardens into fibers. These fibers weave together and form a structure. More cells come along and produce different things. Some make cartilage—the flexible stuff like at the end of your nose. Some cells make bone. What do you need to make bone?"

"Ice cream!"

"Yup."

"Does that mean I have to have it every day?"

"I think, maybe . . ."

"This day keeps getting better, Mom!"

I knew that bones start healing almost immediately after the break.

"Kai, Love," I choked out.

"Not every day?" he said.

"No, Honey, that's not it. I just want to tell you I am *so* sorry I didn't believe you. I am so sorry I dismissed your telling me you thought it was broken. I'm sorry it took me so long to get you checked out and get you in a cast."

I hugged him. Lost in the moment. He hugged me back and then I realized he was wiping his mouth on my shoulder. I looked at him. He grinned. "You have calcium on your shoulder, Mom."

I wept again and laughed.

"Mom, I LOVE this cast! I can't wait for the kids to sign it."

He had his red cast on for four weeks, and it was signed by everyone in school. It's still out in the garage. The thing is in a Ziploc baggie, because it really stinks! I keep it there as a stinky memorial to myself. Not that I need it, because at least once a week for the last four years Kai starts out a conversation like this: "Remember when I broke my arm and you didn't believe me?"

Yes. I'm not about to forget.

=== ⊙ TIE A BONE IN A KNOT ===

Here's a really cool experiment to do next time you have a roast chicken. It will illustrate the importance of calcium for strong bones. And it's fun!

WHAT YOU NEED

- White vinegar
- Clean chicken bones
- A jar with a lid

WHAT YOU DO

1. Put the chicken bones in a jar. Cover the bones with vinegar, and put a cap on the jar.

2. Wait for a week. Check the bones every day and see how bendy they become.
3. When they're bendy enough, tie them in a knot. Rinse the bones and let them dry.

WHAT'S GOING ON?

Bones are made up of hard stuff (calcium) and bendy stuff (soft bone tissue). The acid in vinegar breaks down the calcium, leaving only the flexible tissue.

10

WHAT IF YOU SCREW UP?

ON ST. PATRICK'S DAY, our family has lots of luck; unfortunately, a lot of it is bad. It is marked by accidents and emergency room visits. This time in March comes filled with trepidation for me. I guess it did for Caesar, too. The ides of March. Beware.

Way before Kai and Leo were even a dream, my dad had been driving on the turnpike in Maine feeling drowsy. As he pulled off the road to rest, the car flipped and he was in a terrible accident. He shattered his ankle, his wrist, and his collarbone, and fractured his spine.

It happened on St. Patrick's Day.

One morning in 2007, Keith stood up from putting laundry in the dryer. He did it with gusto, not realizing the washer door was still open. He gashed his face wide open, just missing his left eye.

It was St. Patrick's Day.

Upon returning home one Monday evening in 2008, we opened the door to see that the animals had gone bananas. Oggy had been on a chew-everything spree. He had severed several lamp wires, chewed the end of the couch arm, and gnashed open and swallowed our fifteen-year-old dog Myrtle's arthritis pills.

I called Liz, our vet, and she said to immediately call the poison control number. I did, and before they give you any information they ask for your credit card number. You give it, you pay—and they put you on hold. Their hold line doesn't have music. It has recordings of scenarios. "What do you do when your dog swallows rat poison?" And "What should you do if your cat eats detergent?" Or "If your dog is hit by a car . . ." My level of stress was increasing with every circumstance. . .

When the woman came back on the line, she urged me to take the dog to the emergency care hospital immediately. It's a good thing I prepaid for that bit of advice. Meanwhile the time I took on the phone with this place lost us valuable minutes! Three thousand dollars later, Oggy returned to us—charcoaled, irrigated, and no worse for the wear.

It was St. Patrick's Day.

As a clan, we lose our balance on March 17, for some reason.

In 2009, when Leo was five, he did not disappoint. We had friends over for corned beef and cabbage, and the kids were playing outside. I had been lulled into a late-afternoon sense of security when Kati, who was six, casually came in and reported that Leo was crying and that there was blood.

A lot of it.

They had been playing tug-of-war with an old mop handle they had discovered in a pile of sticks and bamboo poles. These things were usually used for "safe" games like spear tossing and sword fighting.

Unfortunately for Leo, who had been on the losing end of the mop, his end also held the rusty shard of metal, which gashed his hand as Kai yanked the handle through for a win.

Leo screeched.

Kai, thinking he was just being a sore loser, didn't react; but Kati, who had been umpiring the whole event, noticed the blood dribbling out of Leo and reported the drama to the grown-ups.

We were off to the emergency room.

It should be said that Leo has a curiosity about and gentle skepticism for the medical profession based on his abhorrence of getting shots. I was driving with a wailing banshee in my backseat. I made many attempts to quell the panic.

"Hey, Sweetie. After the doctor, we can go and get ice cream."

"Nooooooooo!"

"OK."

We had forty-five minutes to go before we were at the ER. I needed better material.

"What if I need stitches, Mommy?"

"Then you'll get them. It's fine. They'll numb it up for you and you won't feel it. It will pull the sides of the wound together so your hand can heal."

"Nooooooooo!"

"But Sweetie, you may not need stitches. They may use glue or butterfly bandages. Let's wait and see."

"Nooooooooo!"

"I will tell you that even though this is scary to you and it hurts, it's so amazing what our bodies can do."

"What do you mean?"

"How our body heals itself. It's incredible. Can I tell you about it?"

"OK."

It worked! "OK! So it starts with your skin. Your skin keeps your insides in and the outside out. When you cut yourself, there's a hole."

"With LOTS of blood. A hole with lots of blood that hurts a LOT!"

"Yup, that's your nerve endings. They are sending a message to your brain that there's a cut and it hurts."

"Why! Why does it have to hurt?"

"Because your body is telling you something is wrong. It's like an alarm so you'll stop doing what you are doing and take care of this injury."

"It hurts!"

"I know, Bub. Your body is in working order. It's a good thing."

"It doesn't feel GOOD!"

"I know, Sweetie. So your nerves send a message of pain to your brain, and your body also gets other messages. Blood flows out of the blood vessels that are broken. Those blood vessels crush up and try to stop the blood from flowing out of your body. There are these spiky oval cells in your blood called platelets. And they hook up together across the opening of the blood vessels and form a kind of net that acts like a little dam—it's called a clot. The clot can stop the blood. They make a scab.

"The scab then shrinks and pulls the edges of the cut together. In a day or so, other cells, fighter cells, come to the cut and kill off all the bad-guy bacteria that want to get inside your body and party. There's a huge fight, and your good guy blood cells win. More little cells come in and seal up the wound. New cells fill in the gap. Then your skin cells multiply and reach out across and connect. Voilà! The whole thing takes a week or so."

"Am I going to have a scar?"

"Probably."

"Nooooooooo!"

"Oh, Honey, didn't you know? Every scar is a story you can tell again and again."

We had arrived. Leo and I were rushed to a room and a cheerful doctor came right in—after three hours. It had given us plenty of time to make a tongue-depressor dragonfly with tongue depressors and gauze that I found in a drawer.

"Nice to see you, Leo," she said. She smiled warmly.

"It is NOT nice to see you!" Leo yelled.

"I am sorry. He hurts and he's scared," I assured her. I held Leo's good hand.

"I understand," she said to me.

"Can I see your hand, Bud?"

"No!"

"Leo, Honey, she needs to see the cut so she can help get it on the right path for healing."

"You said my skin would already do that, Mom! You said it was in-credible! I don't even know why I am here!"

I laughed and smiled at the doctor, who seemed patient.

"Leo, your cut may be too deep for your body to fix it up on its own. Let's let the doctor see."

Leo looked at me and then looked at her. He offered his hand. She inspected it gently.

"OK, Bud, we're going to need a couple of stitches to fix this up."

"Nooooooooo!"

She continued. "First we need to cleanse the wound and let you soak that hand in a liquid that will numb the area."

Leo energetically refused.

"Noooooo! What about glue or a butterfly, like Mom said?"

"I'm afraid that won't hold up well. This is right on the palm of your hand. You move that part a lot. The stitches will make it better, and it won't hurt. I promise. It will feel a little weird, but it won't hurt."

Leo looked the doctor straight in the eye and yelled, "WHAT IF YOU SCREW UP?"

Suddenly the action in the room stalled. The doctor blinked. I blinked. She looked at me, and I blushed.

"No one has asked me that before."

Leo's courage in the face of authority was both embarrassing and inspiring. Part of me worried that Leo was disrespectful; but then I realized he was just expressing his very real feelings and questioning the world. It was a fair question—one that I would never have dared to ask. I grew up believing that the medical profession was always right, and you didn't question it. I did what the doctor said because he was a grown-up and grown-ups know, right? Leo was a product of a new generation who demanded to know what would happen.

What if she did screw up? It was his right hand. He was right-handed.

"Well, Leo. That's a legitimate question. There is always the possibility that I could screw up because I am human, and these things happen, right? I mean, you didn't intend to cut your hand tonight, but it happened. So all I can say is I will try to do my best. I will put my years of schooling and years of practice and expertise that I have gathered over time and do my very best. I have done a *lot* of stitching in my career, so I know a thing or two. Can you trust me?"

I trusted her.

Leo looked at her.

In a tiny voice, he said, "Maybe."

That was enough. She rinsed it. He howled. More people came in. One guy had earplugs in. She asked me to hold Leo on my lap. I did. Then each adult in the room grabbed an appendage as the doctor told Leo what would happen in a soothing voice.

"Bud, don't look. If you look, it's worse."

This was not a line of reasoning that was going to work. I knew this kid. He began to struggle. The adults held him down. In the loudest voice ever emitted from Leo came:

"I HATE THIS PLANET!"

Wow! Go big or go home. The whole planet?

Everyone laughed. The doctor had to stop what she was doing. She tried to soothe him, but she couldn't help laughing. Even I was laughing.

Leo was not.

New approach.

"Leo, I'm sorry to laugh, but that was kind of funny."

He cracked a smile and began to laugh, too.

"Here's the thing. We have to get this done. Can we try something?"

"What?"

"Remember this tongue depressor dragonfly?"

"Yeah."

"Watch this." I took two quarters from my purse and taped one under each wing.

"It can balance right on the end of your finger, if you're steady enough. All we have to do is find the center of balance. Take a deep breath and concentrate. Are you ready?"

"OK."

"Put out your finger—on your good hand."

He did, and I balanced the makeshift bug. It wobbled, but stayed.

"That's really cool," said the doctor, genuinely interested.

"Now Leo, hold it steady." He concentrated on the dragonfly. I looked up at the doctor. She had already beaten me to it. Because his hand was numb, she was able to put in three stitches before he even knew it.

The dragonfly remained balanced.

"Done!"

"What?" Leo dropped the dragonfly and looked.

The stitching was done.

"Your cut can start healing now, Bud. Hope you don't still hate the planet."

"I don't."

On the way home, we stopped for drive-through milkshakes. They were green. It was St. Patty's Day, after all. We had regained some balance in the storm and found our center. Maybe our luck was turning after all.

BALANCING ACT

Balance is a fun thing to play with. One way to get it is by putting heavy objects in the center and lighter ones farther out. Here's a fun balancing bug.

What You Need

- Cardboard
- Scissors
- White glue
- Glitter, paint, crayons, or markers for decoration
- Two pennies

What You Do

1. Cut the shape of a dragonfly out of cardboard. You can use the template on the next page or create your own. Make the wingspan about 6 inches across.
2. Decorate your dragonfly. Use paint, glitter, googly eyes, or whatever you like to make the bug dazzle. Glue a penny to the underside of each wing at the tip.
3. Balance the dragonfly on its nose on the tip of your finger.

WHAT'S GOING ON?

The center of gravity is the point where all of the mass of the object is concentrated. This is a helpful principle that may entice your children to enthusiastically practice the next time they're balancing on a log or trying to carry multiple dirty dishes from the dinner table to the dishwasher.

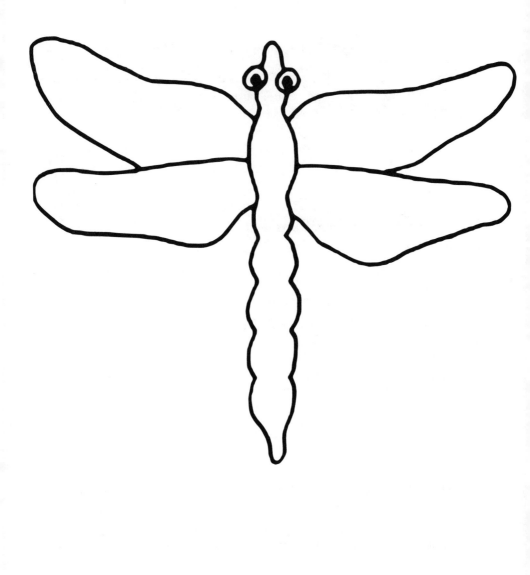

11

NOSE FLUTE AND ARMPIT FART

WHEN KEITH AND I went to Leo's school for our first kindergarten conference, we sat at the small desks and waited to hear glowing things about our darling boy.

The first thing Mrs. Baril said was: "Keith, Leo has been teaching the other kids to—how should I put this—make rude-sounding noises with his armpits. And he does it all the time—standing in line, at recess, even in the classroom. We've received comments from the music teacher about Leo's sounds in class. He calls it music."

Keith reddened, then pointed to me. "That's not me. It's her."

Mrs. Baril lasered in on me. "Lynn?"

What could I say? I laughed.

Wrong response.

So I tried to recover. "It's . . . a . . . skill," I said. "One I do not possess, but one I can teach, and Leo's a natural! It's all about sound waves, you see . . . it's science . . ." I trailed off.

Mrs. Baril twinkled. "It's not about the skill—although I'm not sure it's a building skill to set him up in life—but it is about the timing. That's what he needs work on."

"I understand, of course. We'll talk with him." What I was thinking was *Why isn't that considered music? What is music, anyway?*

The truth is that I believe Leo's conduction of successful experiments with pressure and sound waves, developed through rigorous experimentation, *is* an amazing building skill that *will* serve him well in life.

It all started with a peep in the middle of the night. What parent hasn't been jolted awake by a single chirp from their baby down the hall?

"Mom?"

I am snapped awake and I know exactly who is calling my name in the dark. It's Leo. In the seconds it takes to decrust my eyes and creak out of bed, my brain bolts from an "OhmyGod" to a calm and a comforting "What's up, Love?"

"My ear hurts so loud it woke me up," Leo cries.

I could relate. I remember waking up crying with pain in my ears, and my dad hugging me and telling me he remembered the same pain when he was a kid.

I find a warm, wet washcloth and the children's ibuprofen.

"We'll get it checked in the morning, Honey," I tell him. "I bet you have an infection, a little party going on inside your ear."

"I can't hear right," he says. "It's like I'm under a blanket."

"That's the party, Bud. Those little microbes found a way into your inner ear and set up shop. They make the inside of your ear puff up and close off the ear like a private room. Then they keep growing. That's what you are feeling—the pressure from those bugs becoming more and more crowded in there."

"I hate that party!"

"It's no fun, that's for sure. Those bugs will either go off on their own after your body fights them off—or we'll have to find some help to kick them out. Either way, it *will* feel better. Try to sleep now."

"I can't."

"Try?"

"Can we look at a book?"

Early on, my kids learned the secret trick of postponing bedtime. Lob out the idea of reading a book. They know it will *always* work on me.

"Maybe one about ears?" he says in a small voice.

That seals the deal. I find one—yes, I have books about such things. I can't help myself. I love books about anatomy and bodies and medicine. In fifth grade I'd received copies of *Gray's Anatomy* and *The Anatomy Coloring Book* for Christmas. I got to know my ulna from my humerus, my metatarsals from my metacarpals.

Leo and I snuggle under the covers. We soon become absorbed in all things ear—the two of us with headlamps in the darkness. Leo's ache dissipates under the spell of ibuprofen. Ears: amazing, funny-looking funnels on both sides of our heads that collect vibrations set free in the world.

I begin to babble. He's used to it. I daresay he finds it a comfort. At least, that's what I tell myself. "So, Leo, every time we talk, we push air past our vocal cords, they vibrate, and—tralala!—air molecules are set in motion."

"TRALALA! I'm vibrating molecules!"

"Ooh! We can't see them, but they're right here in front of us, like eensie-weensie bumper cars crashing into each other like crazy and rippling from my mouth. Close your eyes. Can you imagine sound coming out of our mouths, like waves?"

"Kind of. It's pretty."

"I think so, too. Now picture those waves moving along and flowing into the air around us and then getting caught in our trumpet-shaped ears. The ears catch the wave and the wave moves into our ear canals, where the molecules—"

"You mean eensie-weensie bumper cars?"

"Yeah, eensie bumper cars bounce up against our eardrums."

"Ouch."

"No, it doesn't usually hurt; it just makes the eardrums start moving to the groove, you know?"

"Mom, don't dance."

"OK, sheesh. I got the moves, Baby."

Silence. Then laughter.

"Then what, Mom?"

"Then the bumper cars shake the eardrum in a rhythm—*boom boom boom*—at a certain speed. This rattles these teeny-tiny bones—the hammer, anvil, and stirrup. See them here?"

"Cool, they look like the things you find in owl pellets."

"They do! But they're not rat bones. They're our bones, and their job is to jiggle. Jiggle, jiggle, jiggle all day. Vibrations. It's all about vibrations."

"OK, but I still don't see why that is *sound*. How do we hear the jiggling? Your voice doesn't sound jiggly."

I do my best opera whispery high note. Leo covers his ears.

"OK, OK. Well, let's see. Vibrations. They're happening all around us. Let's just stop and listen."

We do. Leo's eyebrows jump at every new sound.

"I hear Myrtle snoring," he says.

Myrtle is our fifteen-year-old dog, who will only sleep if she's within feet of the kids. She trades rooms throughout the night. She snores.

We wait. "Ooh! I hear a car going by!"

"Here's the thing. So there are all sorts of vibrating molecules and waves of sound coming at us from all around, but we can only hear some of them. They're jiggling and rippling at all sorts of different speeds. We can hear the ones that vibrate between twenty jiggles per second— really low sounds—to twenty thousand jiggles per second—really high ones. Sound waves are measured in something called hertz."

"Mine hurts now."

"Funny bunny," I chuckle. "Did you know elephants can hear super-low sounds? That's how they communicate with each other in the wild. They send out such low sounds, we can't even hear them. These low waves travel through the ground and other elephants can pick up the vibrations in their feet!"

"Bats hear high sounds, right?"

"Yeah! They send out high-frequency peeps that bounce off insects and back to the bat. Then they know where to dive for dinner!"

We look at the diagram of the ear. "Ooh, look," I say. "Doesn't that part look like a snail? It says here that it's 'a tiny snail-shaped, hair-lined tube called the cochlea.' When the waves of vibrations pass and wiggle through the fluid inside, the tiny hairs wave back and forth— like seaweed during high tide. Those hairs wake up nerve endings that then send electric messages to our brains. That's how we hear.

The little hairs move, they wake up nerve cells that send an electric jolt to a part in our brain that we experience as sound."

"Huh?"

"I know, it's so complicated and beautiful, isn't it? It's *amazing* that what starts as molecules clacking together outside in the world travel into our bodies and tickle bones, drums, and hairs and fire up nerves that wake up in our brain as sound! Even more amazing is the organization of these waves and signals that settle in our brains as music. And how do we remember music? Let alone reproduce it or even create it?

"What's even more miraculous is that we can store all these frequencies and nerve impulses in our brains and file them away so that we can recall, arrange, and pick out specific sounds—like music and poetry, or your voice, or a cat purring, and all the rest of the wonderful hum and roar of life around us."

Like the gentle sound of the now-snoring Leo, whose "loud" earache or prattling mother were no longer screaming him awake.

I, however, could not sleep. I had chattered my way into a fit of passion. I was hooked on ears and sound and music and *why*. I had a book about ears and sound, and I had my iPhone to track down even more information. Like any respectable geeky mama, I was happy to wander off on a tangent of my own.

And wander I did. This time I found Brian Greene: physicist, string theorist, and all-around rock-star science guy. Among other things, he theorizes that every particle making up atoms (that in turn make up molecules and all the stuff in the universe) starts with a dancing, vibrating filament—or string (thus, string theory). The vibrations have frequencies that are all part of a beautiful mathematical puzzle that comes together in a variety of ways to create particles, atoms, molecules—everything.

So, again, *what* is music? What happens in our brains to make a piece of music move us? The specific speed of vibrating molecules—or strings or barely imaginable filaments vibrating at the very foundation of atomic structures—does something *mathematically* inside our brains and affects us as *emotion*. But how?

Earaches are an unfortunate inheritance, but music is a grand one.

My grandmother was a concert pianist. When I had mentioned this to the boys before signing them up for piano lessons, they couldn't get over that she was a "PEE-a-nist." This was singularly what they took away from piano lessons.

I finally started to doze off, falling into that place where thoughts buzz into flight on their own. Vibrating strings, emotions, music . . .

In the morning, Leo's earache is gone. A blip. In celebration, I pull out my old trombone, which I had been somewhat coerced into playing in middle school when my request to play drums was denied (too many drummers already—which turned out to be a blessing in disguise, as I came to really love the trombone). I dust it off and play a rousing "Take the A Train," then the *Jaws* theme. I sure don't have the chops I once had, but it's worth the puffy lips and red ring. It stirs up the cats, makes Oggy bark, and starts the kids jumping.

The boys clamor for a turn.

Leo blows and blows and finally sings into the instrument.

"How does this thing work?"

"Put your lips together and then buzz them. You have to vibrate them."

He does, and the call of a moose in love emanates from the trombone.

"Yay! I did it! I play the trombone now!"

"Well, kind of."

"SSSFFFFFWWWWWWWWZZZZZZTTTTT!"

"OK, OK. You *can* play! Isn't it awesome how you can just vibrate your lips and then make music out of it?"

"Vibrations, vibrations, vi-BRAY-tions . . ." Kai begins an operatic performance, and Leo blats out notes from the trombone.

This was our Sunday morning sound landscape, set against conversations, traffic, TV, footsteps, heartbeats, laughter, and the various ambient sounds of boiling tea kettles, fingers turning pages, and a cat meowing in another room.

Different things manifest themselves in different sounds. That night, after a day full of bouncing on the trampoline (with its world-beat flavor), playing video games (with its techno feel), and Lego building (with its tweets, clicks, and whirs), I tuck the house in, musing on the small, whooshing sounds of boys breathing and dreaming, a cat wheezing, Keith's thundering snore, a dog barking in a yard up the street, my own breath. I click on the computer for one final check and notice my video camera had been moved. There is a file, so I download it. The boys had made a video.

It opens with Kai in his tighty-whities holding his recorder, with which he'd been in love since second grade. He lifts it and begins playing "Ode to Joy." Yet something's a little off. He's not playing with his mouth. He has inserted the recorder up one side of his nose, and is playing while trying not to laugh.

Suddenly Leo joins him in the frame, also in his undies. He lifts his arm and wedges his other hand under the pit. Then he rhythmically meters out high-pitched armpit farts in tempo to Kai's melody.

They finish. Then they look at each other and then the camera, both giggling. Leo comes over and shuts it off.

It is one of the best versions of "Ode to Joy" I have ever heard, and I will never forget it.

We don't hear with our ears; we hear with our brains. Our ears and our bodies are simply resonating chambers. Where does music come from? The magic of music goes beyond the science of vibrations and frequencies and formulas. It's the genius of the unexpected. Vibrations can come from surprising places: from unseeable strings in every particle of every atom in the universe. And sometimes from a small, upturned nose, an armpit, and a cupped hand.

SEE SOUND

Because all sound is vibration, here's a really fun little experiment to try with your kids to see it in action.

WHAT YOU NEED

- A bowl
- Plastic wrap

- A rubber band
- Small handful of rice

WHAT YOU DO

1. Wrap the plastic wrap tightly across the opening of your bowl. Use the rubber band to secure the wrap. It should be tight like the head of a drum.
2. Set the bowl on a table, and sprinkle a little uncooked rice on top of the plastic wrap.
3. Stand about 5 inches away from the bowl, and talk to it. Sing to it. Hum. Yell. Whisper. Try it from different angles. What happens? Can you make your grains dance?
4. What happens when you sing high notes? Low notes? Loud notes? Soft notes?

WHAT'S GOING ON?

Every sound we make sends a vibration through the air. In this experiment, the vibrations bounce off the plastic wrap and bounce it up and down, taking the rice for a little ride!

PERFORM AN ARMPIT FART

Though this is commonly misconstrued as a daddy-only trick, it is possible for a mama to eke out a small sound, but it takes practice. Start in the pool. It actually works well when you are wet. When you become more adept, you can continue the fun by sliding your hand to your underarm in any environment. I'm right-handed and, it turns out, right-pitted. I can only do this with my left hand and right pit. Follow the directions if you're right-pitted and reverse them if you're a lefty.

WHAT YOU NEED

- Your hand
- Your armpit

WHAT YOU DO

1. Cup your left hand.
2. Hunch your back slightly and lift your right elbow up and out to create a small pocket in your armpit.
3. Place your cupped left hand neatly over the pocket, placing your thumb on the front of your shoulder. There should be an air bubble inside your hand/pit.
4. Squeeze abruptly and swiftly by cranking your right elbow down toward your side and squeezing the air out of the pocket.
5. You should hear a sound. If you don't, experiment with your hand placement.

WHAT'S GOING ON?

Your cupped hand traps a bubble of air in the hollow of your armpit. Making a seal with your hand traps the air. When you force the air out past the seal it vibrates your hand and pit, making a sound.

It doesn't take much to make a simple reed instrument. All you need is something flat that can vibrate against something else. In this case a simple plastic drinking straw will do the trick. With the right cuts and the right amount of air you can transform a straw into a working oboe!

WHAT YOU NEED

- A plastic drinking straw
- Scissors

WHAT YOU DO

1. Pinch one end of the straw flat—as flat as you can. The plastic of the straw will not want to crease flat, but by using your fingernail, you can flatten it as much as possible. From above, the shape of the opening will look like a football.

2. Cut both corners off to form a point (see illustration).
3. Place the pointy end in your mouth and blow hard. You may have to move the straw in and out until you get to the exact spot where the two points vibrate and you make a sound.
4. You can make different pitches by placing holes down the length of the straw. Try two holes at first. Cut a small diamond-shaped hole by snipping at an upward angle, and then meeting it with a downward-angled cut.
5. Place your fingers over the holes and play. Lift up your fingers, and place them back over the holes to hear different notes.

WHAT'S GOING ON?

By cutting the end into a point, you have two flaps that vibrate when you blow air past them. You have made a double reed! Reed instruments work by vibrating a wooden reed in the mouthpiece.

You can get different notes by changing the column of air. Shorter columns make higher pitches. If you put a hole near the top and leave it uncovered, the air column is shorter, so the note will be higher.

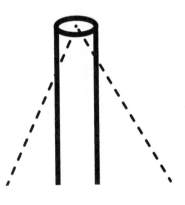

12

LICE MAMA

IT WAS A LOVELY early morning in the Pacific Northwest. Foggy, warming. Spring was a promise in the air. Parents gathered at the bus stop with mugs in hand, and kids scrambled up the trees. The birds were singing, bugs were buzzing, and people were full of good cheer.

The bus dragged its caterpillar-like body up the main drag and hissed to a halt in front of us. The buses on Bainbridge are retro—of course they are! They are picturesque, like enormous Twinkies on wheels. The kids jogged across the street—backpacks whacking their backsides in unison with each footfall. We sipped our coffee, smiled warmly, controlled our well-behaved dogs on their leashes, and waved to our perfect children.

A mom sidled up next to me and whispered conspiratorially. "Hey, I just wanted you to know that there might be, although only *possibly*, perhaps be a small, no-big-deal outbreak of lice at school—specifically Leo's class; but you *didn't* hear it from me."

I waved to Leo and he waved back from the window on the Twinkie bus. As if on cue, he started scratching his head. The other moms took a gentle and friendly step back. They had been listening. Everybody listens when someone whispers!

My head started to itch, too; but I was determined not to succumb.

"Lice?" I said with a nervous giggle. "I didn't hear anything from school."

"Oh, they're everywhere. They can't get them out of the carpet in the kindergarten room, and when the kids go into 'cozy reading corner' and put their little noggins together, the lice have a field day. It's a BIG problem in Leo's class. I know for sure there was a girl on the playground with the little things just hopping off her head. Her mom is one of those all-natural types and doesn't believe in killing the lice with anything harsher than mayonnaise. But you *didn't* hear it from me."

"Mayo?" one mom said. "Seriously?"

"We've never had it," said another.

"Neither have we."

"But I hear it's a problem. And really, there's no shame in it. It's not a reflection of how clean or dirty you are—from what I hear."

The conversation bubbled around me.

Lice!

Even worse—*secret* lice!

Even worse than that, I did what any self-respecting Bainbridge Island mom would do when faced with the possibility of a nasty parasite infection. As the back of my head seared with a tingle, calling me to drag my fingernails across my itching scalp, I ignored the itch and I deftly denied the possibility of lice.

Not *my* family. Yuck!

The thing is, as soon as she said it, I *knew* we had it! Lice had simply not been on my radar—ever. Leo *had* been scratching for a week, and so had I. I thought my shampoo was too drying, or that maybe my laundry detergent was irritating the back of my neck. All good (and very clean) reasons for scratching your head.

But lice? *Ew!* Visions of medieval paupers, street people, and Dickensian waifs with no loving homes wafted through my tingling head. Panic began to simmer. I could go home and soak everything in insecticide, or I could lean on my old friend Science and see what I could dig up.

First, I looked up *lice.*

There are a zillion sites dedicated to the identification and removal of head lice.

Some have cute names like *Lice to Know Ya!*, *Hair Whisperers*, *Miami Lice*, *Rapunzel's Secret*, and *Nit Wit*. I went directly to the Centers for Disease Control.

"*Pediculus humanus capitis*, the head louse, is an insect of the order Psocodea and is an ectoparasite whose only hosts are humans. The louse feeds on blood several times daily and resides close to the scalp to maintain its body temperature."

They're bugs.

They are parasites, which means they live on a host and cause it harm.

OK, I thought, nothing new.

Lice are about the size of a sesame seed. That almost makes them sound cute. Sesame seed cute! Ha! Look closer. They are a milky beige. Lots of ugly things are milky beige.

Lice have six grasping legs, with a single sharp claw at the end of every appendage. This helps them grasp the hair shaft—and grasp they do.

They have swollen, segmented abdomens. Females cement their eggs onto a shaft of hair, near the scalp. The eggs need the warmth of the human scalp in order to incubate and develop. They are tiny white spots. Called nits, they can hang out on a hair for about a week before hatching into nymphs—adolescent lice. I can only imagine the attitude of an adolescent louse.

One of the signs that you might have head lice, according to the CDC, is the feeling that something tiny is scampering around on your skull. The nymphs are scampering! Again, it sounds almost cute. It's not.

Nymphs look just like adult head lice, but they are about the size of the head of a pin. Because they are insects, their skeletons are on the outside. They have to molt and shed their skin before they can grow. They do this three times in one week, and at the end emerge as an adult.

Ew.

Then there's the itch. A louse's tiny, sharp mouthparts slice into your scalp and suck the blood right out of you. *That's* what itches. Their slimy saliva is filled with an anticoagulant so your blood will flow. They need to have a blood meal several times a day. They can live for thirty days on your scalp before kicking it. The females can lay up to eight nits a day. So in a month, one louse could make your head pretty crowded, with 240 possibly viable nits waiting to hatch—and they lay more nits.

That's just one! They all grow up and lay more eggs. The math is staggering.

If an adult louse wanders off the host's head—I think it's funny to call your head a host; it's not as if you're actually throwing the party— it crawls because it cannot jump. It can creep to a scarf, a hat, or a pillow, but unless it finds a new scalp to explore, it will die within a couple of days.

I read all about how lice are drawn to the cleanest of heads. They are passed around when kids exchange hats or put their heads together. Or, as in Leo's case, when they roll around on the infested carpets in the book nook and cuddle corner.

Lice are just doing their job—making a living, having kids, and try- ing to survive. Unfortunately, they do it all on our heads—and only our heads. For some reason, they don't hang out on dogs or cats or even on other parts of our own bodies—though I was horrified to read that sometimes they can lay their eggs on your eyelashes and eyebrows. They like a good, clean, warm place to live.

Really, they're just like any living things. Except they're gross and they carry with them a nasty stigma. What parents want their kid to be the "lice kid"?

Was Leo the lice kid?

Did that make us the lice family?

Did that make me the lice mama?

The horror.

I e-mailed Mrs. Baril and asked if she'd seen any itching or any signs that Leo had lice. Could he go to the nurse and be checked? She wrote back that she was instructed to tell me that unless he has actual lice on his head or was complaining, he could stay in school.

What? That wasn't my question. No wonder they had a problem.

She also said they were not allowed to send kids home or even send out a message—apparently an effort to spare parents the humiliation of having their kids pinned with an unpleasant label.

When the boys got home from school, I channeled my inner monkey and went through their hair in search of the elusive lice and their apparently easier to spot nits.

I could see no nits, but I still knew something was up; so we went to the doctor. Actually, we were going that day anyway, so when Dr. England was just about to have Leo say "ah," I said casually, "He may have lice—how can we tell?"

Dr. England recoiled.

"You recoiled!"

"Did I?" he asked sheepishly, and laughed.

"You're a doctor *and* you have kids and you *recoiled*!" I said, trying to laugh my way through the moment.

"They're icky."

"Well, yeah, that's true."

"I have LICE?" Leo interrupted. "COOL! I want to name them!"

"Let's take a look," said the doctor. He snapped his hand into a rubber glove, took a pencil and a light, and gently lifted a section of Leo's hair. He looked. Suddenly he winced and recoiled again, this time dropping the pencil.

"He's got it." Then he made an "eww!" face.

Leo, however, had an elated face. He was psyched. "AWESOME!" he spouted and began spitting out possible lice names: "Pygmy, Scout, Itchy, Scratchy, Digger, Chomp, Lil Bit . . ."

Meanwhile, I was thinking, if you are a doctor, are you *ever* supposed to make an "eww!" face? Especially when all the websites I saw and the parents at the bus stop that morning assured me there was "no shame in head lice."

If there was no shame, then why was our doctor so desperate to get us out of his office? Why the wince? I pretended I did not notice this time.

"You're going to want to shampoo everyone with that nasty lice shampoo and then pretty much wash everything in the house," he said.

Then he looked at Leo and Kai.

"Don't share hats with anyone, and put your jackets over the back of your chair at school."

Then he looked at me.

"Been to the movies lately?"

"Why, is there a *Lice Monster vs. Tokyo* flick I shouldn't miss?" I laughed. He did not laugh. Instead, he grimaced.

"You can get it at the movies because people hunker down and put their heads on the upholstered backs of the chairs. You come along and lay back and *woomph!* You've got lice."

"Woomph?"

"Yeah. Nasty, huh? OK, so have a good weekend and let me know if you have any questions."

As we left the doctor's office en route for the cleaning of a lifetime, my head spun. How many surfaces do our heads actually contact in a day? The car seat, pillows, couches, hats, scarves collars, towels, blankets, sheets, stuffed animals, animals. I was feeling the power of organization and plan of attack coming on. Bring it on, lice! I'll take you down!

Kai interrupted quietly from the back. "Mom, don't tell anyone, OK?"

We had lice. But in a world where this kind of thing doesn't happen out loud, the outbreak was to be kept secret. There was something deeper happening here.

"Oh, Honey!" I said. "You didn't do anything wrong!"

"I *know* I didn't. But I don't want everyone knowing we have bugs on us. It's gross. What will they think of me?"

"They'll think you're a bug garden—a bug arena, a bug ecosystem!" piped up Leo. "It's SCIENCE!" he said, as if he were announcing a monster truck rally star.

"Well, Honey, here's the thing . . ." I started in.

"Here we go," I could hear his eyes roll.

"I think we got the lice for a reason."

"Because we're gross?"

"Not exactly. I think we got it because other people are ashamed of it. So they didn't say anything and we caught it from them because we had no warning. They are ashamed of the idea of lice because it carries a bunch of bad ideas with it."

"What?"

"If you are embarrassed about something because you think it makes you unworthy or unlikeable, you hide it. You make it a secret. You push it under the rug."

"You get lice from under a rug?"

"Kind of. The fact that no one said anything made us vulnerable in a way because we had no reason to protect ourselves against something we had no idea was lurking out there."

"But how come *we* got it? How come *we're* the ones? It's not fair."

"Lice isn't fair! Get it, life isn't fair. Lice . . ."

Kai was silent and about to tear up in the back. Why do these things always happen in the car? I parked.

"Are you crying?" asked Leo incredulously.

"NO!"

I reached back to hold his hand. "Listen, Love, here's a cool opportunity for us to be courageous and maybe even make a difference for someone else. If we tell people we have it, then they can plan. We didn't *create* the lice."

"Yeah, that's eggs," said Leo. "Or is it mama lice. Heh! Which came first, the lice or the lice egg?" He waggled his eyebrows.

"We didn't start the lice outbreak, but we could help stop it, maybe."

"How?"

"Well, we take care of our problem first." I paused to scratch my head. "We shampoo, we comb, we clean; we stick everything that will fit into the dryer, and the rest we seal in plastic. We take these lice down."

"Down TOWN!" said Leo. "S'up lice? You're going DOWN!"

Kai cracked a sideways smile and glanced at Leo. "S'up lice? Really?"

"Then we tell folks," I continued. "We don't keep the stupid secret that there are lice. We destroy the power of the secret shame of lice. Are you with me?"

"*Yes!*" hollered Leo.

"I guess," said Kai, a little less enthusiastically.

We drove home. Despite the myriad "natural" treatments, from mayonnaise to oils, unguents, and various citrus rind, I had been reading about all morning, we took a triple-threat approach.

We began with chemical warfare. We all shampooed with creamy lice-killing shampoos. Then we launched a fire-and-brimstone campaign on anything that might have come into contact with any of our heads. It turns out ten minutes in the drier is enough to kill lice and nits. Keith was able to stuff unbelievable things into the drier. We unleashed a physical assault last, by combing and picking and blow-drying. No lice, no nymphs, and no nits had a chance. We were victorious.

Our scalps tingled with clarity, truth, and triumph. Our house sparkled. It had taken a whole day, but the battle had taken its toll. I was sure we had managed the problem.

Then it was time to use my words. I wrote an e-mail to parents of all the kids in both Kai's and Leo's classes. I called my friends. I explained that we had contracted lice and embattled them and won. I encouraged them to keep an eye on their scalps. I considered it a brave and courageous act. I was self-righteous.

It wasn't even a minute after I pushed *send* that the phone rang.

"Honey, it's for you," Keith said, bringing the phone to me. He had a weird look.

"Hello?"

"Hi Lynn. It's Bev. You have lice? How awful for you. Can I drop off a casserole?"

I thought she was kidding.

She wasn't.

I knew her kid probably had it as well. Everyone had it! She was never going to admit it. She was reveling in our misery. It's way better to watch someone squirm than to be the one squirming. Oh God, what had I set my kids up for? *Lice!* It was now defining us. *Ick.* Even the doctor winced!

The phone didn't stop ringing. The moms at the bus stop riddled me with questions. E-mails flooded in. Everyone wanted to know how I faced the demon lice and lived. Parents I didn't even know stopped me in the grocery store. "Lice mom! You're the lice mom, right?"

Lice mom? Like a superhero. Or an action figure. Lice Barbie—her arms bend so she can reach her itchy scalp!

"Can you look at my daughter's hair? She's been scratching. Show the nice lice lady, Honey."

People at the gym stopped me "Hey, you had lice, right? I heard. Can you tell me if this is dandruff or a nit?"

I heard myself spouting off comments like, "Actually, more kids get head lice than all the other communicable diseases all added up—you know, except for colds." People would nod—from a safe distance.

But I sensed they were grateful for the information. Somehow in my zeal to teach my kids how to take the high road and take responsibility, I became the town lice expert. Even though I postured to the kids that we had done the right thing, deep down I was embarrassed. I was horrified, and I felt judged.

The drama all happened on the parental front. We can be so judgmental when in fact it's the virus, or the bacteria, or the louse just doing what organisms do—making their way, replicating, and finding the best way to survive. Just like us.

The kids were fine.

Leo never once thought any part of the whole lice saga *wasn't* awesome. He loves insects, and he delighted in the science of their life cycle. He learned about parasites and communicable diseases. It was a great springboard for him.

I decided to embrace Leo's thrill of the revolting and take it on in all its disgustingness.

We're not perfect, though we spend so much of our time trying to make ourselves seem so. We do this to ourselves by dieting and training for triathlons and spending obscene amounts on clothing, or by sucking the fat out of our butts and injecting it into our face, or by not allowing ourselves to delight in pasta, chocolate, or any other decadent pleasure for fear of adding pounds. We work to have the "perfect" kind of house and furniture and yard and car and job and relationship and kids.

Can I possibly even consider myself a decent parent if we all got lice?

Yes.

The nerd gift that lice brought to me was the realization that my job as a parent was *not* to tell my kids they were perfect. I am not perfect.

Keith is not perfect. Life is not perfect. Perfection is too much pressure and is all about secrets and show. My job is to tell myself and my kids: You are imperfect, and that's what makes you beautiful.

You hold that itchy head up high.

You are authentic.

You are real.

You have lice.

Admit it.

Embrace it.

And zap those suckers.

Is your head itching yet?

JAM JAR TERRARIUM

Make a jam jar terrarium and grow your own cast of nasty little critters—maggots, earwigs, mold.

What You Need

- Glass mason jar with lid (I used an old spaghetti sauce jar)
- Potting soil
- Activated charcoal (sometimes called terrarium charcoal)
- Small stones, pebbles, or gravel
- Moss
- Plants (such as ferns)
- Decorations (such as small toys, larger rocks, etc.)
- Chopsticks

What You Do

1. First, prep your jar by washing and drying it and removing any labels.
2. Add a 1-inch layer of pebbles to the bottom of the jar.
3. Sprinkle a thin layer (1/4 inch) of charcoal to help filter the water and absorb odors.
4. Add a 3- to 4-inch layer of potting soil. If you want to make a mountain, mound up the soil in one area.

5. Add the plant life. Place pieces of moss in a single layer inside the jar. Use chopsticks to move the plants around, adding plants like small ferns and whatever you find. Try it. Decorate with rocks, shells, plastic toys, or whatever you like! Water the plants, then add the lid.

6. You will need to water your terrarium every few weeks. Droplets of moisture are fine—you *want* to see these—but if it starts looking especially foggy in there, take the lid off for a few hours to let moisture escape. Otherwise, an occasional water and/or spritz with a spray bottle should be fine.

7. Find some insects if you like, and toss them in. Ants are a good bet. Close the lid and watch them in their environment. Or leave it insect free.

13

ON THE BRINK

KAI CAME IN at around 4:00 A.M. and poked me to wake me up.

"I don't feel good, Mommy," he said as every single ravioli that he had consumed for dinner erupted in magnificent force.

Usually Keith does the puke scene. I, unfortunately, usually add to the puke scene by gagging violently. It was a big concern for me when I was pregnant. Not because I had morning sickness—which thankfully I did not—but because I knew I was a buddy booter (one who tosses her cookies at the first sign of someone else doing so) and I was worried that I wouldn't be able to handle the inevitable children-puking scenarios that were bound to occur.

And occur they did. One of the most memorable was the time we were on an airplane descending into Seattle for a landing. Keith had little baby Leo on his lap. He was fussing, I thought, because of the pressure. Keith held him out to me.

"Feel his forehead. Does he feel hot to you?"

At which point Leo let loose and threw up down my cleavage inside my shirt. Handy for airplane cleanup, yes; but I was stunned silent.

Keith took Leo back.

"Sorry, Honey."

I stayed frozen in one spot until the UNFASTEN SEATBELTS came on, and I grabbed Leo and mama-tigered my way off the plane to the bathroom to clean us both up. Thank God I didn't puke back on him. Sheer will.

I was revisiting that sheer will on that fateful night. The good thing was that Keith was home. So I rolled over and groaned "Eeewww, Honey! Can you help?" I stifled some gagging.

"I'm sick," is all Keith said. I could tell he meant it.

So I did it. I cleaned up poor, shaky Kai and put him back to bed. I got the carpet cleaner out and I cleaned up the offending mess. I showered and disinfected everything I could lay my hands on. Keith slept.

At that point it was time to get Leo off to school and kick into high Dr. Mama mode, making appointments at the doc for Kai—and for Keith, who still couldn't drag his butt out of bed.

In our society, we are told to muscle through the illnesses we get. Take cold medicine and keep working; blow your nose and get on with life. You think you can ignore it and it will go away. Sometimes it does. Sometimes it doesn't. Now I know why it seems like sickness hits men harder than women: only because my experience is that my husband actually slows down and takes care of himself when he's sick. Do I resent it? Well, yes; but I do admire it as well.

I didn't really resent it in Keith this time. He had been sick with a sinus infection for the better part of a year, and our lives had spiraled into cuckoo-bananadom lately with a series of illnesses and deaths in the family. Keith had been working hard and picking up the slack while I traveled to various funerals and bedsides.

Now the holidays were upon us. Who had time to be sick?

First, I made the appointment for Kai; then, I made the appointment for Keith. I told Keith it was in an hour. He said he could drive, and I scooted off to drop Leo at school and take Kai to the doctor's. While I was in the office with Kai, who had the flu, my phone gurgled. I ignore the phone in the doctor's office. Call me crazy. When I got out, I put Kai in the backseat and he fell asleep in an instant. I checked my phone. It was a burbling Keith, saying faintly, "I am too dizzy to drive right now; can you change the appointment until this afternoon?"

I called him up. I was Madam Fullcharge. Something took over. He answered and I said, "The hell I will cancel this appointment. You get your clothes on and scoot down those stairs on your ass and I will take you to the doctor NOW."

He did, and I transported the greenish, sweaty mass of a man to the doctor. I knew he probably just had the stomach flu, like Kai; but I was worried.

I told them he might be sick, and immediately they whisked us into a room. Our doctor came in and looked at him. She listened and she took his temperature.

"This is serious," she said to me. "I think he has pneumonia and sepsis."

"Pneumonia and sepsis? Don't you die from those?"

"You can. He needs a chest X-ray and a blood draw. Go down the hall."

I had to help Keith walk down the hall. He was staggering like a drunk. There was no way we were going to wait in any line.

This was the same person I became when Leo puked down my shirt on the airplane. I didn't care whom I pushed past to get there; I needed to do something for my baby.

An older woman came to take his blood and told him that if he felt dizzy to put his head between his knees.

"With all due respect, if he does that I think he'll fall on his head."

Keith stood up unexpectedly, and the older woman and I rushed in to flank him. It was as if the marionette's strings were snipped. He sagged and dropped.

We made it to the bed.

Mayhem broke loose.

People were everywhere.

The doctor came back. "Which hospital do you want to go to?"

"Uh, uh, uuh, the closest?" The nurse behind the doctor shook her head, making meaningful eye contact with me. "The best? Seattle?" The nurse behind the doctor nodded her head violently *yes* when I said Seattle.

"He may not make that," the doctor said.

Now I was dizzy.

Kai was asleep in the car. Keith was unconscious, and I couldn't make a decision.

The paramedics saved me. They had halted the ferry, swept Keith up, and whisked him via ambulance to the front of the ferry line and off to Seattle. Before they left, I remembered to tell them that Keith is allergic to so many antibiotics. I pressed the list I carry in my wallet into the hands of the paramedic, whom I recognized from the annual pancake breakfast. He hugged me and told me it would be OK.

I was numb; but I kicked into a high gear of capability. It was easier than thinking about what this might mean. To Keith. To the kids. To me. So I sent out the word to Dad and my friends and straightened out who would take care of the boys so that I could go. I leaned out—away from my own, independent core—and reached beyond. I was scared. I tumbled blindly, and my friends and my father caught us without question as we fell.

Everyone stepped up.

Keith began the fight of his life. When I got to the hospital he was in so much pain he was almost delirious. His legs looked like that wine-marbled cheese you get at holiday time. "Why are his legs like that?" I asked.

"They're not always like that?" said the doctor.

More mayhem.

One nurse came in and gave me a copy of *Sepsis News*. Sepsis News? She asked me to wait out in the waiting room.

I wandered like a zombie and sat down with *Sepsis News*. On the cover was a handsome young white doctor who looked reassuring and capable. He had a stethoscope around his neck and a calm smile on his face. I liked him.

I read on.

> Sepsis, or septicemia, is a life-threatening illness that can occur when numerous bacteria in the blood are actively dividing. The whole body reacts to an infection. There may be organ dysfunction. There may be shock. The heart may stop. Seventy percent of people who get sepsis die. . . .

I dropped the page and went right back to Keith's room. I wanted to be there if anything like that was going to happen to Keith.

In the meantime friends took care of the boys, made meals, cleaned the house, did the laundry, called, and visited me in Seattle.

It felt safe to feel unsafe. It was the greatest gift.

Six long days.

Keith pulled through. He thinks it was no big deal; but it really was. We almost lost him.

He remained in the hospital, but I came home after he was released from the ICU. I needed to see the boys, and I knew they would want to know what was happening.

I've always felt comfortable communicating even the hardest concepts to my kids; but this one stumped me. We are such small potatoes. How fragile we are. How do you communicate this fragility to young kids during times of turmoil? Or do you? What do they need to know to stay secure in an emotional whirlwind?

They really wanted to know. They didn't want the watered-down version.

"He's fine, guys. He's good. He's been in a battle, but he won."

"What kind of battle?" asked Kai, wide-eyed.

"Kind of a bug battle. You know how Daddy's been blowing his nose and coughing a lot lately?"

"Yeah."

"Well, the little bugs that were causing that sickness all kind of got together and waged a war. They wanted to take over. But they didn't."

"How does that even happen?" asked Leo.

I said what I always say when I don't know. "Good question. There's cool science, there."

I scooped immodest amounts of ice cream into three bowls and we snuggled on the couch and debriefed.

I told them how colds and flu are mostly caused by viruses—which are tiny and icky. I have never found anything good about viruses. They are interesting, for sure. They are like mini-robots that get into your body and use the stuff in your body to make copies of themselves. They make you sick and eventually your body kicks them out.

But bacteria are different.

"Wash your hands!" Leo squawked.

"True. Bacteria are *everywhere*."

"Wash EVERYTHING!" cried Kai.

We all screamed until we laughed.

"We have been taught to hate and fear bacteria," I told the boys when we calmed down. "Antibiotic rinses, antibiotic soaps, lotions, detergents, sprays, wipes, and kitchen and bathroom cleansers make promises to eradicate the evil bacteria that lurk hither and yon. But here's the thing. Some bacteria are bad. Truly bad. But some are actually good, and mostly they do good things. They hang out on us and in us, and because of these bacteria, we can make vitamins, digest our food, and fight bad germs.

"In fact, if not for bacteria we'd be up to our eyeballs in trash and waste. We wouldn't be able to digest anything, plants wouldn't grow, and we'd be totally unprotected from diseases caused by viruses, fungus, and other untold little nasties."

"So we *want* bacteria?" Leo asked.

"We don't have a choice. We're actually more bacteria than we are human."

"No way," said Kai with a mouthful of Cherry Garcia.

"Way! You are human and I am human. That means each of us has about a trillion human cells that make up our bodies. But there are *ten trillion* bacterial cells in you and me and on you and me. That means we are ten *times* more bacteria than we are our own cells."

"You just can't wash that kind of math off," added Kai.

"Nope, and you wouldn't want to, either. We need them to be alive."

"I'm a bacteria city—BACTERI-OPOLIS! AHHHHH!" Leo threatened Kai.

Kai ignored him and pressed me. "So how come if bacteria are good, and we're practically bacteria cities ourselves, how come Daddy is in the hospital?"

"Some bacteria cause trouble."

"Like that mean kid, Brad?" he said. "He picks his nose and steals stuff."

"Brad has challenges, yes, but he's not out to get you."

"Ride the bus with him and then see if you want to say that."

"Some bacteria do terrible things. They have no business being in or on you. They make you sick.

"The bacteria that landed Daddy in the hospital were everywhere inside Daddy. There were gazillions of them. They started out as one, ate, grew, split in half to make two, and then they grew, split in half, and each made two until there were so many of them they caused havoc."

"But they're so little. How can they do anything at all—good or bad?" asked Leo.

"Leo, Brad's pretty little too, and he makes all sorts of bad things happen," said Kai.

"Well, they're too small *on their own* to make any difference; but when there are a ton of them, they send out chemical messages to each other and then they all attack together. That's what gets us in trouble."

"That's what happened to Daddy?"

"Yup. To a bacterium on its own we are *gi-normous*. It gets in and it waits. It eats, it multiplies, and when there are enough of them, they launch an attack. I read all about this in a magazine the doctor gave me."

I remembered *Sepsis News* with a shudder. While I loathed its bedside manner, *Sepsis News* had actually become a fascinating friend, keeping me occupied while Keith slept. I learned all about the behavior of bacteria to recognize the self from the others; how they use chemicals as a kind of language to activate group behavior when the numbers of organisms were high enough to make a difference. It's called "quorum sensing." Though I hated them for doing this inside of Keith, I was mesmerized by it.

As I tucked Kai and Leo in that night and waited until they and their personal bacteria cities fell asleep, I wrapped my own bacteria-riddled arms around my bacteria-swaddled self and allowed myself to cry for the first time.

I felt overwhelmed by everything. By the fear and the fact of it all and how easily things can be knocked off balance.

The tears were as much about relief and gratefulness as anything. I was relieved Keith was alive. I was relieved that the antibiotic the hospital chose was the right one the first time around. I was reminded how small we truly are in the great scheme of things, and how easily things can become derailed. After all, to us it just appeared that Keith had a bug—until *whomp*, he fell off a cliff. Who knew it was all about quorum sensing?

There were so many what-ifs that could have led to disaster that didn't.

Then there was the quorum sensing of my own tribe. I felt cradled by all the friends who rose up in the wave of our emergency. How lucky were we to have come upon and cultivated those friends as the fabric of family that we can form. We are hardwired for tribe and are blessed by the interconnectedness of community that is essential for helping every single one of us weather the weather.

I took a shower and rinsed a few populations of bacteria from my skin. Bacteria have been around on this planet for billions of years, and people have only been puttering around the planet for a couple hundred thousand. We're not so different. Yes, as humans, we're bigger and have a few more bells and whistles than bacteria; but there's something to learn from these tiny forces of nature.

Together, we are able to do things that we couldn't possibly do on our own.

💡 GROW YOUR OWN GERMS

Make your own petri dishes with "germ food" and see what's growing in and around us.

Culturing microbes (bacteria and fungi) on petri dishes lets you test different surfaces for microbes and grow your own germs. It's also a great reminder of why it's important to wash your hands. Even very young children will have fun helping with the cotton swabs and seeing what grows in their microbial zoo. It's fun and easy, and you might even already have what you need in your kitchen cupboard. If not, the ingredients are readily available at any grocery store.

WHAT YOU NEED

- Disposable clear containers to grow cultures in (we used clear deli containers)

- 1 beef bouillon cube or 1 teaspoon beef bouillon granules
- 1½ packages of plain gelatin or 1½ tablespoons agar-agar (agar-agar is a seaweed gelatin that can be found with Asian ingredients in some grocery stores)
- 1 scant cup water
- 2 teaspoons sugar
- Cotton swabs

What You Do

1. Make the germ food! Mix together the water, gelatin (agar-agar), bouillon, and sugar. Bring the mixture to a boil on the stove, stirring constantly, or boil in the microwave, stirring at 1-minute intervals and watching carefully until the gelatin or agar is dissolved. Remove the boiling liquid from the heat and cover it with aluminum foil. Let the growth medium cool for about 15 minutes.

2. Make your petri dishes. Pour the medium carefully into clean containers, until they are one-third to one-half full. Loosely place lids over the containers, and allow the dishes to cool completely. The gelatin or agar should make the growth media hard like Jell-O.

3. When the material in your petri dishes has hardened, store the dishes in a cool place, like a refrigerator, until you're ready to use them. Use the dishes in 2 to 3 days, and when you are working with them, try to keep the lids on loosely whenever possible so they are not contaminated by the air.

4. Label the dishes. Decide which surfaces you'd like to test. (Fingerprints are cool, door handles, broccoli, keyboards, phones, and so on. You can even cough on one or leave it open to the air for half an hour to see what's floating around!) Then, draw a grid of four sections on the bottom of the dish with permanent marker. Label each section with the surface you want to test. If you picked clear containers, you should be able to see through the gelatin to see your lines and your writing.

5. Get your samples. Rub a clean cotton swab around on the surface you want to test. Then, remove the lid and gently rub the cotton swab across the section labeled for that surface. If you are careful, the gelatin shouldn't break. If it does, it's no big deal. Put the

dishes on a flat surface with their lids on. Check them every day, and soon you will observes colonies of different shapes, sizes, and colors starting to grow.

WHAT'S GOING ON?

You will mostly see fuzzy spots. These are likely fungi (molds). You may also see some tiny clear or white spots that are colonies formed by millions of bacteria. They're everywhere! Look. Be amazed, and then throw them out. Don't open the lids!

Wash your hands! If you wash your hands with regular hand soap for the length of time that it takes to say the ABCs, you'll remove most of the harmful bacteria and viruses on them. (You also might have the sudden urge to disinfect computer keyboards and remote controls.)

14

HOW WAS SCHOOL TODAY?

THE BOYS ARE IN SECOND and fourth grade. It's the last year they'll be in the same school building until they're both in high school. They ride the bus together. My schedule is wrapped around theirs; forty-five minutes before the bus is to come home, I hitch the dogs up and go for a walk through the woods.

During the walk I anticipate seeing the boys. I wonder about their day. I shift from writer-mom to mommy-mom. After a day of just writing, I look forward to talking.

When the bus crests the hill and slows with a hiss, the conversations among the parents halt as the kids pile off—arms loaded with bags, papers, and jackets (if we're lucky; the lost and found at school is a veritable gold mine of kid clothing).

Every day when the boys step off the bus I enthusiastically ask, "How was school?" Seriously, *every day* I do this. I am sincere; I want to know.

The answer is always the same: a glazed "Good" from each boy as he comes near for a brief hug and we wander back home.

You'd think I'd learn.

I do not.

I narrow my research questions. Broad, open-ended questions are difficult to wrangle. Everyone knows that. Specifics . . .

"What was the funniest thing that happened today?"

Various grunts and shoulder shrugs.

Still too open-ended. I have to be more sensitive to the "coolness" factor. I wait until we're not within earshot of anyone—except the dogs.

"What specialist did you have today?"

"Art."

"Cool! Both of you?"

"Yup."

Now we are getting somewhere.

"What project are you working on?"

"I don't remember," said Leo.

"Yeah, I don't know," said Kai.

This is when things start to spin out of control for me.

"You don't remember? Weren't you *there*? I mean, were you crafting stained-glass windows? Making mechanical puppets that walked by themselves? Did you—"

"No, Mom. I don't know. Something with hands," Kai says, exasperated.

"Leo?" I ask.

"Ayuno," he shrugs.

I change my tune and chat about the snack I will prepare them. "How about sliced apples dipped in peanut butter and granola?"

"OK."

"You guys tired?

"Uh huh."

"OK, we can chat about it later."

"Hey, Mom?"

"Yeah, Love?"

"I get an hour of screen time, right?" Kai says earnestly.

"Yes."

"Me too?" chirps Leo.

They dash off down the road to home after depositing their bags and papers on me, and I walk home with Oggy and Myrtle on leashes, a couple of backpacks on one arm, papers and jackets under the other arm, and a couple of poop bags in my hand.

It's not pretty. It's not how I dreamed of communicating with my kids. I chalk it up to an uneventful day. They happen.

Later, when I visit my friend Jill, her daughter, Addie, who is in Leo's class, gives a very different and articulate discourse on Leo's day.

"There was a substitute teacher and she was *mean* and made Lulu cry and then we had a field trip and we walked to the farm and it HAILED and then when we got there we harvested potatoes and Peter took a bite and THREW UP and then the farmhouse suddenly CAUGHT FIRE and there were alarms and the fire trucks came and put out the fire with a huge hose and there was mud and sirens and everything and then Leo got in trouble for playing King of the Mountain on a pile of TRASH and the principal saw and YELLED at him and now he has to have lunch inside with the principal ALL WEEK and in art we got to THROW POTS on a wheel and I made a bowl that I turned into a kitty and it was totally awesome."

I look at Leo.

He looks at me, smiles, and nods.

"Like she said."

Addie looks at Leo and then at me. "He didn't *tell* you?"

"Alas, Addie, he is a man of few words."

"Yup," Leo says. "Hey Addie, I'll race you down the hill!" and they both run off.

I must have looked adrift, because Jill laughed. "I get it all. If you ever want to know anything, ask me; Addie's got a direct line on everything."

Lord knows I, like Addie, can provide a running commentary on just about anything. Language is something I use frequently as a tool for processing. I talk it through, and when someone asks me how things are going, I take that as a sign of them caring. For me, language becomes a way to express not only news but admiration and love.

Was it just me and my brain? Is it a girl thing? How do male and female brains process things and use language? What strategies can we harness to make sure communication channels remain flowing? How can I teach my boys why I communicate the way I do, and why they communicate the way they do? Is it biology? I had to know.

The first free moment I had, I started digging in. I remembered an article I had read in a science magazine awhile back and started there. It talked about how brains differed between the sexes. Men's brains were bigger than women's brains. This spawned a whole host of theories in the turn of the century about how women couldn't handle academe because of their smaller and therefore assumed "inferior" brains.

Ha!

Then it turned out that male brains were bigger because the ventricles (cavities within the brain) were bigger, too. Bigger brains, bigger holes in the brains. This stuff was too good *not* to share. I found Keith.

"Keith, this is cool. Our brains are really different."

"Duh."

"Seriously, men and women may have basic biological differences that could explain why communication is difficult sometimes."

"Honey, are you from Venus?"

"Very funny, Bugs Bunny."

"Are you going to make me read that book again? *Please.* I don't need to read the book. Honey, I love you. I cherish you—"

"You *don't* have to read the book. Listen. So, women have neurons in their brains that are packed in really tightly, like a bunch of sardines. Because there are a lot of them and they're close together, they 'talk.'"

"I am shocked."

"Impulses can travel super fast between neurons. The neurons are most dense in certain layers of the brain responsible for language and communication. Even on a cellular level, we're zippy communicators."

"Makes sense. Honey, how long is this going to take? Can I set the table?"

"Keith! This is interesting!"

The boys tumbled in. It was dinnertime.

"OK, but the kids and I are hungry and I promised them we'd play games at dinner."

"Games! Yay!" the boys cheered.

"Some scientists did imaging studies on male and female brains to see what was going on when people did different things. When men were asked to do a language task, a certain small area of the left side of the brain lit up brightly. When women did the same task, the whole brain lit up like a Christmas tree."

"So women have a superhighway and men have a donkey path? Nice."

"Mom! Are you calling us donkey heads?" Leo was always concerned about verbal insults.

"No, Leo. I'm talking about how brains are different. Keith, both men and women did the task equally well, they just used their brains differently. There's more than one way for a brain to come to the same conclusion."

"That's what I'm talking about. No, wait. Why are we talking about this? And can we talk about it later?" Keith changed the subject and said to the kids, "I'm thinking of an animal."

"Is it a mammal?" asked Kai.

"Yes."

"TAPIR!" hollered Leo.

"No."

Dinner was a wonderfully boisterous affair with back-to-back games of "I'm thinking of an animal" and jokes and "I'm going on safari." My boys had no trouble talking and processing this kind of information. But I wanted that shiny picture of family bliss where we share our days over plates of healthy organic homemade meals that everyone loves. Instead it's komodo dragons and Crock-Pot chili and no mention of anyone's day.

Later, when the boys were getting ready for bed, Keith and I were washing dishes. I was churning.

"Honey, what's wrong? You are uncharacteristically quiet."

"Ha-ha."

"Seriously."

"It's the boys! They *never* talk about their days. I find everything out from Addie. Today, Leo went on a field trip to the farm, a kid threw up, the farmhouse burned down, and Leo got in trouble and has to have lunch with the principal for a week, and all I got when I asked how his day was, was 'good'!"

"It does sound good. A week of lunches with the principal . . . wow."

"I want details. I want them to share. I want them to know they can tell me anything. I want open communication so they'll talk to us when they're teenagers and—"

"Honey. They won't. Not when they're teenagers. They know they can, but they won't! At least, not the way you want it to happen."

"*Not* helping."

"They're like me, Lynn. They need time to let the experiences trickle through their brains. You'll see. Tonight, when you tuck them in, you'll get them talking. Don't bombard them with questions. That's your superhighway zooming. Let them come to it. Remember. They have a donkey path, like I do."

I decided to try Keith's way. I tucked Leo in and reached for the book to read.

"Mom, the fire engine was really awesome . . ."

We spent the next twenty minutes talking about his day, including how unfair the principal was and how he really was king of the mountain. Keith was right. I didn't prod. I didn't ask leading questions. I just allowed Leo to talk, on his terms. We wandered the donkey path, and it was lovely.

That night, in the dark, my thoughts ramped up. I whispered to Keith.

"Do you think we can rewire how we are wired just by trying? Do you think we can come to a middle? Accepting the science of it is a great way to accept and embrace differences and attain a Zenlike compassion for the processing of others, but I don't want to have a 'boys will be boys' moment and allow it to be an excuse for not teaching the kids to communicate clearly. Is it something I should try to change? Is it something I could change? Or even should change?

"I do know that Kai and Leo take the path of least resistance. So do I for that matter. I have to make an effort to fight the good fight.

"It happens in school, work, and life. Bump up against a subject that's hard and fast, you dislike it and then you chalk it up to 'I'm no good at this.' Happened to me with chemistry and economics. I let it slide when I was younger because I wasn't good at it. But now I know I have to redouble the effort when I bump up. I may not like it, but it's good for me, right?"

"Uh huh," said Keith.

"Is it the same with teaching the boys to talk more? Maybe it's easier to just not talk about it."

"You might consider that one, Honey."

"Is it all in our heads? If maybe I could boost their confidence with communicating they would embrace it. I know a lot of girls that chat and talk about their days. AND I know a few boys, so maybe it's not a black-and-white boy/girl thing. But what it is might be a genetic thing. Our boys, it turns out, communicate like you, Keith. Is it because they watch you and mimic you? Or is it a genetic predisposition? Can we overcome our biology, or are we fated to fulfill these genetic prophecies?"

No response.

"Are you asleep?"

"I want to be."

"Keith! Don't you think this is something to discuss?"

"I think you are discussing it because I think you are processing it. I value your process."

"Thank you, but . . ."

"Did Leo talk to you?"

"Yes, but—"

"Did he do it on his own terms?"

"Yes."

"Can you value his process?"

"Yes, but—"

"Why are we still talking?"

He had a point.

"You have a point. I love you. Good night."

After all these years, I am still stunned by the economy of how Keith processes information and experiences. He does not need language as a way to get closer and figure things out. He sorts things out on his own and uses language to communicate when it's necessary *after* the figuring out. When I ask him how his day is, right off the bat he says, "Good." I often learn more about his day when he tells a story days later. I found myself lost in translation. His way frustrated me. My way frustrated him. I used to be insulted by this, and I'd badger the poor guy to talk more. Surprisingly, this did not work.

Now, being the mature woman I am, I see that he needs time to process in his own way. He, being the patient, loving man that he is, allows me to chatter and process verbally. I see my own boys processing and using language so very differently than I do. I am also beginning to see that I need to adjust my approach to communicating with them.

They need time.

In my zeal to help Kai and Leo grow up, I often forget that I, too, am on my own path of growing up. Loving someone is giving them what they want, how they want it—with no strings attached (within reason, of course). It doesn't matter whether or not we're wired for it biologically. What matters is what *works*.

It's my lesson to learn, not theirs. It's me who needs to try and rewire.

We're all clopping along our own donkey paths.

I secretly wonder what part of my brain lights up when I realize this.

══💡PILLOW JOURNAL══

Create a private journal for translating the processes of boy brains and mama brains and keep the communication open. This is a simple book to make out of paper, cardboard, a stick, and some rubber bands.

You need heavyweight card stock for the covers. Finding just the right card stock can be a fun thing to do together. We've used Lego boxes, old game boards, old book covers, cereal boxes, even corrugated cardboard.

WHAT YOU NEED

- Heavyweight paper or card stock for the cover
- Paper for the inside pages
- A twig the length of your paper

- A rubber band
- A hole punch
- A ruler
- A pencil

What You Do

1. Cut your paper and card stock to the desired size. I used college-ruled paper with holes already punched. It's a good size. How many pages to include in your book is absolutely up to you. I think we started with about fifty sheets. Cut two pieces of card stock, cardboard, or recycled box to the same size as your paper.

2. Make the holes. Flip the cardboard over so the front is on the table. Take a piece of hole-punched paper and make a mark on the top and at the bottom where you will need to make a hole. Punch a single hole at each of your marks so that you now have a hole toward the top of the cover piece and one toward the bottom. Repeat the process with the back cover. Punch holes in the back cover piece.

3. Bind the book. Grab your stick. Make sure it's about the same length as your cover. Stack your cover and inside pages in the order that you want them for the finished journal, carefully lining up the holes. Loop one end of your rubber band around the top of the twig and poke the other end of the rubber band through the hole at the top of the journal from front to back. Turn the journal over and pull the rubber band through the top hole. Stretch it down to the bottom hole and thread the end of the rubber band through the bottom hole. Flip the book over again and pull the rubber band through the hole in the front. Wrap that end around the bottom of the stick. The book should be bound now, and the twig should be lying flat along the left edge of the front of the book.

4. Decorate the cover as you wish. You can even glue an envelope on the inside cover for stray bits of treasures.

5. Now make the first entry. Write a little love note asking how their day was. Leave it on the pillow with a pen and see what you get.

15

BABY TALK

It always happens when I'm driving—usually when I'm in a hurry or with my mind on whatever twenty things I need to accomplish in between running the shuttle service for the boys. This time we were on our way to the grocery store. I had a window and decided to drag my nine year old with me. It's never a pleasant experience to bring a nine-year-old boy to the grocery store, despite my best efforts to make it "fun!" a "challenge," or a "learning experience."

I do try.

"Kai, look at all the 'candy' cereals they put at your eye level. Why do you think they use cartoon characters?" or "Find me a rainbow. I need carrots, beets, spinach, and summer squash . . ." or "Can you find the bread with the most fiber?"

We were on our way when he asked.

"OK, Mom. How DO babies happen?"

"Happen?" Oh no, was this *that* moment? Where was Keith?

"You know. How do you make a baby?"

"Oh. You want *this* talk. You want it now?"

"Well, yeah."

"OK . . . so . . ." I gathered myself. "So you know that boys and girls are different . . ."

"Mom!"

"OK, but there's a reason. Do you know why they're different?"

"Um . . ."

Then the horse stirred in the barn and got ready to run. Grab the reins, Lynn.

"The best way I can describe it is this. Remember DNA—the little road maps—the directions or instructions for you in every one of your cells?"

"Yeah, I remember—like when we did that experiment the last time you made pea soup. With the dried peas and dish soap and stuff?"

"Exactly! We saw the DNA—the hugely long molecules with all the directions for making stuff like hair, eyes, ears, and all that stuff."

"Hair on peas? Ew!"

"You know what I mean, wise guy. OK, so every single one of your cells has forty-six chromosomes—those are packets of DNA—they're the directions. Every single human cell has forty-six. *Except* for one special kind of cell in men and another special cell in women. The guys' special cells are sperm—you have them percolating in your testicles."

"Ew! Mom!"

"Well, you asked, Bud. OK, so for women, the special cells are eggs."

"Like chickens?"

"Yes, but waaaay smaller. We have them in our ovaries—two little organs tucked on each side of the uterus." I glanced back to see Kai gazing thoughtfully out the window. "You with me?"

"Uh . . . sort of."

"Inside the sperm and the eggs there are only twenty-three chromosomes. They each have half of the instructions. So when they come together—it's like shuffling the deck of cards. You get twenty-three direction capsules from your mom in the egg and twenty-three direction capsules in the sperm from your dad."

My gaze darted back in the mirror, trying to read his face. He was still looking out the window. I went on.

"Put the sperm and the egg together and shuffle it all up, and each shuffle makes a different set of directions. If it all goes well, the sperm and egg combine and start the process of a new person. Together the egg and sperm now have forty-six chromosomes and starts dividing and turning into a person. This is called 'fertilization,' and the fertilized egg sticks and settles into the walls of the uterus in the woman and the baby develops. It stays there, kind of cooking, until about nine to ten months later, when it comes out as a baby."

I was feeling very pleased with myself for being clear and straightforward. Taking a science approach seemed to be making this stuff easier to talk about.

"OK, Mom, but HOW do the egg and the sperm get together?"

There it is. Stay calm.

"Oh boy. OK. So you have a penis, right?"

He snickered. "Yeah!"

"And it's all hooked up to your testicles, and when you're a grown-up you'll have sperm inside, ready to come out. It's almost like a squirt gun."

"Really?"

"Kind of. A man puts his penis inside a woman's vagina—women have an innie and men have an outie. They fit together. The sperm is shot inside and they swim up and one lucky sperm finds one lucky egg and BOOM! You shuffle the deck and if all factors are working you start a baby."

I'd made it through!

"Wait a minute. Wait a minute, wait a minute. People DO THAT?"

"Well, yeah."

There was a long pause.

"Ew."

He paused, doing the math. "YOU and DAD did that?"

"Well, yeah."

"TWICE?"

"Uh . . . yeah, but when you're a grown-up it doesn't seem so shocking. You will mature—you will go through the magical changes."

"I know, Mom, the magical changes of puberty. But I am never doing THAT!"

I started babbling. I couldn't stop myself. "You'll know when the time is right, but it will be about love and respect because it's a big deal and when you fall in love make sure that you live your life! You'll go to college and live a life before you settle down and have a baby and you will respect women and you will be safe and protected and—"

"Can we get ice cream?"

I took a breath. "Did you hear me?"

"Yeah. Can we get ice cream?"

We have a family tradition of getting ice cream after every painful doctor visit—after the flu shots, after throat swabs, after vaccines. Maybe this talk was as challenging to receive as a vaccination.

"OK . . . Do you have any questions? You know you can ask me anything."

"I know, Mom."

Silence

"Mom?"

"Yes, Love."

"Can we get ice cream?"

PEA SOUP DNA

DNA is an extremely thin molecule averaging about 2 nanometers in width. A human hair is approximately 80,000 nanometers wide. We're talking thin! But you can actually see strands of these molecules without a microscope in this simple kitchen activity.

WHAT YOU NEED

- Handful of dried green split peas
- 1 cup water
- Blender
- Strainer
- Medium-sized bowl
- Pinch of table salt
- 2 tablespoons dish detergent

- Small clear glass
- Meat tenderizer
- Cold, 90 percent or higher isopropyl alcohol (put this in the freezer for an hour before you start the experiment)

What You Do

1. Put the water and the dried peas in the blender, and whip them up for about 20 seconds on high until they are completely blended into a green frothy liquid.
2. Strain the mixture into the bowl, making sure no chunks of peas make it into the bowl.
3. Add the dish detergent and salt to the bowl, and stir gently for 2 minutes. Let the mixture sit for about 5 minutes.
4. Fill the small glass about one-half full of the green goo. Add a pinch of meat tenderizer, and stir for 15 seconds. Use the corner of the paper towel to pop any bubbles you see.
5. As gently as possible, slowly pour cold isopropyl alcohol into the glass until the glass is almost full.
6. Take a look at the white, stringy, frothy mixture in the glass—that is your DNA! (You may need to let the solution sit for several minutes before the DNA becomes visible.)
7. Try the experiment with other fruits or vegetables to see if you can see their DNA. How do they compare?

WHAT'S GOING ON?

The blending breaks the cell open; the soap and salt release the DNA from the nucleus; the meat tenderizer prevents enzymes from breaking down the DNA; the DNA is not soluble in alcohol, so it comes out at the water and alcohol boundary. If you try extracting DNA from other fruits or vegetables, you might see that certain fruits and vegetables seem to produce more or less DNA.

So how can you see DNA when it is 40,000 times smaller than a human hair? Well, the DNA you are seeing is not an individual strand but a tangled mass of all the DNA that is present in a cell's nucleus.

Very awe inspiring!

💡COMBINATION ICE CREAM

We're all about the combinations! Every single one of us is a combination of DNA from our parents. You can drive this point home by making a comforting batch of ice cream to serve when you finally break the news of how the heck babies are made.

What You Need

- 1 tablespoon sugar
- 1/2 cup milk, cream, or half-and-half
- Your favorite things to combine (There's no wrong answer—though tuna is never a good choice here: Chocolate and cherries? Blueberries and vanilla? Pretzels and coffee? Marshmallow and graham cracker? Peanut butter and banana? Whatever it is, start with about 1/4 cup of the stuff and use your taste buds to direct you from there.)
- 1 pint-sized Ziploc bag
- 6 tablespoons salt
- 1 gallon-sized Ziploc bag
- Enough ice to fill the gallon-sized bag halfway
- Spoon

What You Do

1. Put the sugar, cream, and flavorings into the small Ziploc baggie, and zip it up tight. Make sure there are no leaks.
2. Put the small baggie into the big baggie.
3. Place as much ice as can fit in the big baggie.
4. Add the salt, and zip up the big baggie.
5. Now slosh the whole thing around. Massage the bag so that the yummy stuff in the small bag keeps moving.
6. In about 5 minutes the mixture should appear thick. Keep sloshing until you get to the freeziness-texture you like for ice cream.
7. Open up the big bag and take out the small bag.
8. Open the small bag and enjoy!

WHAT'S GOING ON?

While you might want to talk about how two flavors combine to make a new unique flavor, you can also talk about the science behind the freezing part of this project. Regular ice isn't cold enough to freeze milk or cream into ice cream. Adding salt to the ice lowers the temperature of that mixture just enough so the milk and cream will freeze.

Pretty cool!

16

SUNSHINE AND FREEDOM

"Mom, smell my armpit!"

Something every mom loves to hear.

Especially upon awakening.

Kai had entered our room wearing his boxers only. It was 6:30 A.M. on a Sunday morning. Keith was still snoring.

"I don't want to smell your armpit. I can smell you from here!"

"I KNOW! Isn't it AWESOME?" Kai arched to sniff and grinned at me.

"Well, Honey, you are ten now and your body is changing . . ."

"I know! The *magical* changes of *puberty*." He came close for a cuddle, pulling his lanky legs up into a ball so he could snuggle in under the covers. Keith snoozed on. One cat at the bottom of the bed voiced a complaint but never opened her eyes. Oggy stirred in his bed, and in a matter of minutes, Kai was sound asleep.

Propped awkwardly on my side, I glanced at this man-boy. This beautiful being. Hair sprouting off the top of his head in wild angles. Freckles dotting the bridge of his nose. Eyelashes impossibly long.

His breathing was even and deep. Was it so long ago he was only the length of my arm?

Now, to have been awakened at the announcement of a sign of growing armpits. . . . Puberty. Already? I needed to know more so I could be ready (or at least pretend to be ready) for the changes that were imminent in our household.

I used every ounce of yoga knowledge to pretzel my way out from under the covers and out of bed without disturbing anyone. Miko meowed briefly, ending with an innocuous open-mouth breath of a meow.

I made tea. Went outside and sat in my favorite chair and watched the morning unfold. Nalu, the black lab from next door, came along sniffing and wagging her tail. She let me scratch her ears for a while before heading back to her yard to keep an eye on her chickens.

I sipped. The neighborhood was quiet. The sun was up. It was a warm, pink August morning. It wasn't long before I heard a kind of chortling-cooing sound. A mother pheasant and her three growing babies paraded across the yard in front of me, picking at the grass as they went. By the size of the chicks, I could see it wouldn't be long before they would be off on their own. Two of the chicks had begun sprouting colorful male markings. A white ring was blooming around their necks, and their backs and breasts were a coppery chestnut color. Their tails were lengthening and starting to look striped. The third chick was still a mottled brown, like the mother.

They, like Kai, were on the cusp of transition.

Bet their armpits (or wingpits) didn't smell.

School was right around the corner. We had some serious "man shopping" to do.

Along with picking up the traditional school supplies, like ruled paper and adult scissors (that could actually cut), we needed to get some body-maintenance products.

This was a job for Keith. Which is what I told him when he joined me with a cup of coffee.

"Why is Kai in our bed?"

"His armpits stink."

"OK. Maybe I haven't had enough coffee yet, but I don't get the connection."

"He's starting the journey, Honey."

"That *magical journey* into puberty?"

"That's the one."

"What do I do?"

"You have to take him man shopping."

"We have to buy a man?"

"Funny. *We* have to make sure he has body wash and deodorant. He needs to start taking care of his body in a new way."

"Deodorant? He's ten!"

"He is starting to smell."

"Awesome."

"That's exactly what he said this morning when he thrust his armpit into my face."

"Honey, *you* are awesome."

"Thank you, Love."

"Do *I* stink?" He lifted his arm. "Ooh! Time for man shopping, indeedy. So what are we looking for?"

"Good question. I've been doing some reading."

"Here we go!"

"I found some interesting stuff."

"You have a knack for that. Hang on, Sweetie. I think I need more coffee first."

Later that day, the four of us pulled into the parking lot. We had our lists. Pencils, backpacks, water bottles.

"Mom, you should maybe get all that stuff while Dad takes us to the man aisles," Leo chirped in helpfully.

"I think we can do it all together. Besides, I am curious."

"About what?" Kai asked.

"About what's out there as far as products. What's at your eye level? What are they trying to sell you, and how? Plus, I imagine these things all have perfumy smells. I'm curious to see how they smell."

"You can *smell* them, first?"

"You *should* smell them. You're going to be wearing it."

"I want deodorant, too!" said Leo. "I want to smell like Cody."

"Cody smells awesome," said Kai.

"Cody *is* awesome. I want to smell like him and grow up and have a cool job like him and have an awesome girlfriend like he does."

"Leo, it's not because he has good deodorant that he has Marika as a girlfriend and a job at Microsoft."

"I know, but he smells *good*."

"Dad, why do armpits smell bad?" asked Kai.

"You should ask Mom," Leo said.

"Thanks! Am I the expert? Do I stink?" I said.

"You *know* stuff," said Leo.

"It's true," said Keith. "Ask your mother. That's my motto."

"OK Mom, why do pits stink?"

"Cause you *sweat!*" Leo shouted.

"Yeah, but there's more to it than that. *Everyone* sweats. It's actually a good thing. You sweat because it's a way of cooling your body down. You have two different ways of sweating. One kind is through your eccrine sweat glands. They're all over your body and dump sweat right out onto your skin. When your body gets hotter than normal, your brain tells your eccrine sweat glands to send fluid out onto your skin through these tiny holes called pores. The air evaporates it and cools your skin—which cools your body—which makes your brain happy. The fluid is sweat. It's mostly water and salt. Sweat on its own doesn't smell a lot. But there's another kind of sweat gland in your pits and in your groin . . ."

"GROIN? What's a groin?" asked Leo.

"It's your *crotch*, Leo," said Kai.

"Your *groin* is your *crotch*! Ha ha ha! You're *kidding*, right? *Groin* means *crotch*! It sounds like a spring. Groin groin groin!"

"Leo!"

He broke off, laughing so hard that Keith and I laughed, too. All four of us laughed until we couldn't breathe.

When we recovered, Kai said, "Wait. You *sweat* in your groin? Icky. Do I have to put deodorant there?"

"No, Honey—"

"Wait a minute, *crotch sweat*! Seriously?" Leo hollered to gales of laughter from both himself and Kai. Even Keith laughed.

"Guys! We're in the parking lot of Wal-Mart. Please don't scream *crotch sweat*, Leo."

The things you hear yourself say as a mom.

"Anyway, yes, you sweat there. You'll get hair down there and in your pits, and at the base of those hair follicles you have a different kind of sweat gland called an apocrine sweat gland. They dump sweat out at the base of the hair. This sweat is a little different. It's a kind of fatty sweat."

"Aaaaaahhahahaha! Mom you're *killing* me!" Leo barely squeaked out between guffaws, "Groin. Crotch. *Fatty* sweat! Hahahahahaha!"

"OK, when you're done . . ."

"Ahahahahah . . . heehee. Hahaha . . . OK. Sorry." Leo tried to keep a straight face. So did Kai. So did Keith, for that matter.

I waited.

"Aaaaaahhahahaha! Hahahaha."

All of them.

"OK. OK. We're done."

They collected themselves.

"OK, so this sweat happens when you're stressed in some way. The gland, which looks like a ball of yarn, gets squeezed and it spits up a mixture of fat and sweat onto the base of the hair. This is like a banquet for the bacteria that are living happily on your skin. They gobble it up and break it down. That's what stinks."

"So it's like bacteria poop?"

"Sort of. It's kind of cool and gross—like most things."

"So how come Leo doesn't stink? He sweats more than I do."

"My bacteria don't poop! HA!"

"Well, that's not exactly it. He does have bacteria on him—we all do—we need them. But Leo's young. His apocrine glands haven't kicked in yet. That happens when . . . ?"

"Magical journey," Kai deadpanned.

"You got it! During puberty, your apocrine glands kick in. Sorry Leo—no fatty sweat for you yet, my love."

"OK, so how does deodorant work then?"

"Well there's deodorant and antiperspirant. They do different things. Deodorant helps you not smell by making the environment under your pits uninviting for bacteria. Some have chunks of salt that may make the place too salty for bacteria to survive. There are products that make it too acidic. I have even heard about people using lemons."

"Lemons in the pits?"

"It could work. They also have chemicals that kill off bacteria, neutralize the smell, and some even go one step further by adding a scent."

"And the other kind?"

"Antiperspirants. We don't need those yet. Those have chemicals like aluminum chloride or hydroxybromide that squeeze into the pores and make those glands swell shut. That way they don't allow your skin to sweat at all down there. No sweat, no bacteria party. Lots of people have ideas that this might be bad for you in the long run. They think these tiny molecules might lead to cancer or Alzheimer's disease, but there's no real proof. Still . . . Today we stick with deodorant."

We had reached the aisle in question. Leo opened and sniffed everything he could reach. When he got to a Speed Stick, he stopped short.

"What is it, Honey?"

"This is deodorant?"

"Yup. Speed Stick. Funny name, isn't it? It doesn't *scream* deodorant, does it?"

"Last year when I was at David's, we found this in his dad's room and we rubbed it all over ourselves to make us run faster!"

"Did it work?"

"Maybe. But no."

"Probably a good idea *not* to do that again. Though it would have been cool if it did work. I'll bet lots of Olympians would have used it!"

"Yeah!"

Our attention was drawn to other products with names such as Swagger, Game Day, Pacific Surge, Delish!, Bitten, Man Power. They all sounded like they promised something other than killing bacteria on the skin.

There were products created especially for nocturnal animals, the "red zone," and "high endurance." They all appealed to the inner animal and athlete, evidently; but my favorite—as I fought a headache brought on by too many scents released in that aisle that day—was the line of deodorants that boasted *how* they smelled. One claimed to smell like "sunshine and freedom." Another like "guitar solos and triumph" and yet another like "ice and wind." Do any of these things actually smell good? Guitar solos? To me that sounds like it would smell of nervous sweat, bar smoke, and leather.

After some careful searching and sniffing, Kai finally settled on smelling like sunshine and freedom.

Why not?

After an overly enthusiastic application in the car on the way to dinner, we extracted a hazy promise from Kai, with windows wide open, never to apply more than one swipe a day. Too much of anything—even sunshine and freedom—can be overwhelming. It was a good lesson.

I can still taste that sunshine and freedom, since it permeated my dinner that evening as I sat next to Kai. I broke a sweat gazing at this maturing boy embarking upon his magical journey.

He had chosen well. I think a little sunshine and freedom will go a long way and serve him well along the road ahead of him.

YUMMY HOMEMADE DEODORANT

It's kind of fun to make your own deodorant. The ingredients are all easy to find online or at a health food store. I like this particular mix of scents. Plus, these oils are good at killing stinky bacteria. This batch is just like summer and happiness! Feel free to play around with the essential oils to create your perfect scent. Call it what you will. Perhaps you will come up with something that smells like victory and sand or report cards and Tuesday. Who knows?

What You Need

- Muffin tin liners
- Muffin tin
- 1 tablespoon beeswax shavings (this helps keep things unmelty in warm climates)
- Clean glass jar

- Bowl of hot water
- 1/2 cup coconut oil (this has antibiotic properties)
- Chopstick
- 1/4 cup arrowroot powder (this is a thickener)
- 1/4 cup baking soda (this kills bacteria, too)
- 5 drops rosemary essential oil
- 5 drops tea tree oil
- 5 drops lemon essential oil

What You Do

1. Put 2 or 3 muffin tin liners in the muffin tin and set aside.
2. Melt the beeswax in a glass jar standing in hot water. Add the coconut oil. Stir with the chopstick until they just melt and blend.
3. Take the jar out of the hot water bath. Add the arrowroot powder and the baking soda, and mix well. Add the essential oils, and stir to mix completely.
4. Pour the mixture into the lined muffin cups. Fill about halfway. Let it cool, stirring every few minutes or so until it gets to be about sour cream consistency.
5. Let it harden completely.
6. Keep the yummy deodorant wrapped in tissue paper between uses.

17

I WANT TO HOLD YOUR HAND

HAIR IS BIG in our house right now. Leo had been growing his out and looked like a mini Japanese version of Keith Partridge. It was long, luxurious, and slightly curly. It verged on mullet but didn't sink quite to that level. I have to admit, it was really cute on him. He hadn't gotten to that stage where he flicked his head to the side to keep his bangs out of his eyes. They were just short enough so he didn't have to do that; but the back was long enough that it bounced when he walked.

Kai had been growing his hair out, as well. I think it was to catch the eye of a couple of girls in his class. His bangs were longer and gave him a bit of a shaggy dog–Beatles appearance. Unfortunately, he did have the head-twitch thing going on; it was parted on the side and swept across his forehead. He spent hours getting it just so. "Mom, does my hair look good?"

"Very cute, Honey. Very Justin Bieber."

"*What?* It is *not* like Justin Bieber, Mom! It so *totally* is not like that guy. Not at *all*. Gosh, Mom, kill it for me. *Kill* my hair for me. Is that what you want?"

"Not trying to kill the hair, Honey. Did I say Bieber? I don't know what I was thinking. It is not like that at all. Sorry."

"*Mom.*"

"It's cute, Honey. Your hair is awesome."

"*OK.* Thanks."

This kind of dialogue happens on a loop in our house.

When was that day when this boy became aware of his hair? At ten, he was showing the first signs of puberty. His feet no longer smelled like toast. He was an expert eye roller, and he could sigh like an old movie diva.

The first time that both boys came home brimming with crushes on girls in their class, Leo was in preschool and Kai was in first grade. I knew the girls they liked. I liked them, too. At dinner that night, between spaghetti and garlic toast, I nonchalantly asked the boys what they liked about these girls.

Kai was thoughtful, and looked up at the ceiling as he twirled the noodles on his fork.

"She's nice to me. She shared her Hello Kitty crackers with me. She's funny and she's smart. She never gets any answers wrong in class. She knows *all* the answers and she can draw pigs *really* well."

"A good pig drawer is hard to find."

How much did I love that Kai loved this girl for all the right reasons? She can draw! She's smart and she is funny! He never even told me what she looked like physically. I was so proud. Looks were not his sole reason for the crush! What a guy.

"Can you draw a pig, Mom?"

"Your mother is a great drawer of pigs," quipped Keith and pinched me under the table. "It's why I married her."

"How about you, Leo? What do you like about Anna?"

"I dunno," he said, concentrating on the garlic toast.

"Really? You don't know?"

"Well, she's really adventurous. She's not afraid of getting her hands dirty when we paint, and she makes me laugh. Plus she can run really fast."

I looked at Keith. I thought I was going to cry. *Both* boys had solid, wonderful reasons for basing crushes.

Then Leo added in a gravelly voice out of the side of his mouth, "Plus, she's going to be one BEEEEAAAUTIFUL woman!"

"Yeah!" Kai added "My girl is HOT!"

"Yeah, HOT HOT HOT!" they were chanting.

Things were deteriorating fast.

"Guys! Guys!" I looked at Keith for help, but he was laughing too hard. This only made the boys go further, doing a dance while repeating *hot hot hot*.

Now I was stuck. Make it a big deal, and you make it a big deal.

I was the only woman in the house representing *all* of womanhood to these young boys (and husband), and they *would* respect me. They would respect *all* women. I am woman; hear me roar!

"Guys, you can't talk like that. You don't call girls *hot* at this point in your life—and if they are, it should be because they have a fever or just ran a mile. It's not appropriate."

I killed the laughter—just like the hair. They snickered and gazed conspiratorially at each other as they dutifully ate their spaghetti.

Where did *hot* come from? How did they know about *hot*? What did *hot* mean to them? OK, I know we don't live under a rock; but here was a point at which I thought I could do a little teaching. Make a little difference. Only I had no idea what to say. So I twirled my spaghetti as all three of my guys watched me.

"Isn't 'hot' *good*, Mom?" asked Kai.

Keith looked at me with a smug grin. "Yeah, Mom. I think *you're* hot."

"Ew, gross, Dad!" said Leo.

"You are *not* helping, Keith." Where was I going with this? "I am not a prude, guys. All I want is to make sure you understand that girls and women are so much more than just an appealing or *hot* thing to look at." I was finding my groove, locating my soapbox.

"I love that you noticed all the right things about the girls you like. The smartness, the niceness, the funny-ness, and the adventurous spirit. These are the *important* things. Looks and 'hotness' change over the years. Wouldn't you want to be with someone who you really like to laugh with, talk with, and have adventures with, no matter what they look like? In fact, don't you think that by sharing all that stuff and getting to know someone, they become beautiful?"

The only sound was the clinking of forks on the plates as all three guys ate quietly.

"Yes, Honey, of course. Right, boys?"

"Yup."

"OK, can we watch *Sponge Bob* after dinner?"

Why was I talking? These kids were four and six. Crushes are great. They were talking to us. What was my problem?

From the moment we are born, the world bombards us with media and images and lessons about love and who we are. From how our parents act and respond to each other and the world, from commercials to cereal boxes, books, and movies, we get messages all the time about what's "right" and "acceptable." Like it or not, we form the foundation for future love and healthy relationships from the get-go.

I had read all the articles about how television wrecks kids, and early on Keith and I decided not to be those parents who don't let their kids see TV or have sugar. These are the kids, in my observation, that go crazy when they finally get exposed to it—and they *will* get exposed to it. It's a reality in our culture.

We had always planned on arming our kids with knowledge so they could be strong and smart and navigate their way in the sea of wildness that exists out there.

So we watched TV together, and we talked about it. OK, *I* talked about it. I got them to notice the commercials, and we played a game. The game was that the makers of the commercials want your money, so they try to convince you that you need this thing. They win if you start to believe it. You win if you say, "Interesting approach, but I don't need it."

Sometimes we win, and sometimes the commercials win. My kids ate this game up, and only a couple of times emitted a defeated "Mom! The commercial is winning!" when some particularly enticing Hot Wheel or sour candy explosion zipped across the screen.

We watched *The Wizard of Oz*, and I extolled the virtues of Dorothy—who succeeded by being nice and giving and by becoming a warm and strong leader. We read books with strong female characters. When they became smitten with *Star Wars*, I pointed out that the characters worked together and respected each other, but that I wished Princess Leia had more of a presence and talked about the writing.

We chatted about dialogue in sitcoms.

"Is it funny when that kid puts his parents down?" I asked.

"Mom, it's just a show."

"I know, but the writing is no good. Seriously, would you like any of these characters if you met them? Do you think girls have to be mean and sneaky to get ahead? Do you think boys who play sports are stupid? Do you think mean is the same as funny? *And* if you look at all these shows, the parents are all pretty stupid, aren't they?"

"Mom!"

I know. I know. I killed sitcoms. I also kill song lyrics and make sure they know the difference between good sound and lousy lyrics—sometimes they go hand in hand—but to be aware. I hope the message sinks in.

The message is *think*.

And respect yourself.

And ask questions.

And respect girls.

OK, there are a few repeating messages.

"Mom? *Sponge Bob*?" The boys brought me back into the moment.

I did like that Sandy Cheeks. She was strong, adventurous, and smart, and friendly . . .

"OK."

I wasn't done, though. Keith could tell as we cleared the table.

"The wheels are working, Honey. I can see them. Remember, they are four and six."

Good advice, but I had more questions. I pondered. What are crushes? What is love? Through time, our likes and attractions change wildly. If I had married the guy I thought I loved at age nineteen, I would be married to a gay juggler in London.

Why do we love whom we love—no matter the age? All across the world, throughout all cultures and across all ages, people feel love. Animals seem to feel it, too. We all make choices. We all have preferences. Why?

I needed to check in with Science for some clues and comfort.

I found Helen Fisher, a scientist who studied the science of why people love each other. She took people who were in love and tossed them in an MRI machine and looked at their brains. She also looked at people who had been recently dumped. She studied the patterns of what she saw in their brains.

She discovered there is a biology—and a chemistry—to love.

It is evolutionary. Our brains are wired for this. Crushes happen in the deepest parts of our brains—in the primitive parts of our brains. That makes sense. For as long as humans have walked the Earth, we have looked for love. In the deepest regions of our brains, desire motivates us to focus on finding mates for help in partnering to raise babies and continue the species. That makes sense, but it doesn't shed any light on why we choose whom we love.

It's chemical—the attraction part, the love part. It's all chemical. When we have a crush on someone, chemicals are released into our brains and bodies that make us feel joyful and happy and great when we are around that particular person.

Despite the biological and chemical reasons for crushes and love, why are we drawn to particular people? Is it because we're like them? Or we are the opposite? Or is it simply a chemical mystery of smell and sight and sound? Or is it physical somehow? Is attraction actually magnetic?

As interesting as this was, it wasn't going to help me. It wasn't a conversation to have with the boys, yet. Now all they want to talk about, or fuss with, is their hair.

I still can't stop thinking about attraction and forces and magnets and electricity. So when the wind blows, fly a kite, right? The next day, when the kids got home from school, I had a bag of new combs for them—and an idea.

"If you're going to have cool hair, you should have a few cool hair tricks up your sleeve. Watch this, guys," I said.

I took a comb and combed through Kai's hair about ten times in a row. "I'm building up a charge here by loading up electrons—teensy, charged particles. Watch what they can do."

I turned on the faucet to just a small trickle. Holding the comb close to the water, but not touching, we watched. The stream of water bent to reach toward the comb.

"AWESOME!" both kids screamed. "Let me try!"

I gave each kid a comb and set them free to see what kinds of things they could attract. Paper, balloons, bubbles, hair, glitter (somehow we always end up with glitter). With their charged combs they find that, just like love, they are drawn to some things and not others, but exactly *why* may be just a mystery. A delicious mystery that is fun and captivating.

I watch them and realize something. When we turn our attention to the magic of things we emerge as our best versions of ourselves. Along the way there are biological and chemical pulls and pushes, some hotness and coldness, and a little electricity. But in the end there is always abundant and persistent sparkle.

WATER BENDER

You can use static electricity to magnetize ordinary things. Brushing a comb through your hair can charge it up and make it pull on paper, water, even bubbles.

WHAT YOU NEED

- A faucet with running water
- A comb
- A head of hair

WHAT YOU DO

1. Turn on the faucet and slowly turn down the water until you have a very thin stream of water flowing.
2. Take the plastic comb and brush it through your hair ten times.
3. Now slowly bring the comb close to (but not touching) the flowing water.
4. The water bends toward the comb *without* it actually touching the water!

WHAT'S GOING ON?

Stuff is made up of atoms. Atoms are made of smaller parts. One kind of part is an electron. When two objects are rubbed against each other, some of the electrons from one object jump to the other. The object that gains electrons becomes more negatively charged. When you brush a comb through your hair, electrons collect on the comb. Now that the comb has a negative charge, it is attracted to things that have a positive charge. Like water or paper or anything else that might be made up of atoms (everything!).

When you bring the negatively charged comb near the faucet, the negative charges in the water are pushed away and the positive charges are pulled toward the comb. This pull is strong enough to bend the whole stream.

PAPER PICKER-UPPER

This is a cool way to use static electricity to make bits of paper dance!

WHAT YOU NEED

- Tissue torn up into confetti-size pieces
- A comb
- A head of hair

WHAT YOU DO

1. Place confetti-size pieces of tissue on the table.
2. Comb your hair ten times fast.
3. Hold the comb over the confetti (don't touch it); see if the confetti leaps to the comb.

WHAT'S GOING ON?

The paper can't sit still when you place the charged comb over it. The electrons are drawn to the positive charges in the tissue. They can't stay away from each other. The pull is so strong it carries the tissue with it.

BUBBLE MASTER

Try using a charged comb to control the movement of a bubble.

WHAT YOU NEED

- Bubbles
- A comb
- A head of hair

WHAT YOU DO

1. Blow some bubbles into the air.
2. Comb your hair ten times fast.
3. Hold the comb near a bubble. Can you control its movement?

WHAT'S GOING ON?

You know what's going on. The negative pull of the electrons pulls on the positive particles in the bubble and makes the bubble pull toward the comb.

18

A KNIGHT IN SHINING CARDBOARD

I HAVE ALWAYS LOVED HALLOWEEN. Loved the costumes, the night-dark-slightly scary time with everyone you know but don't because they're someone else running around, and the candy—gotta love the candy. I like the chocolate with something crunchy inside. It can be Twix or KitKat or Snickers or Baby Ruth. It has to be chocolate and crunch. It's the only time of year to be specific about such bounty.

Mostly I liked the trappings of Halloween—the buildup. I love carving pumpkins. I love the fall air and watching the leaves turn and walking past the dried-up piles of leaves that collect themselves against curbs and tree trunks. I like spooky ghost stories, dry-ice fog, fake blood, and mulled cider. I like the gak—that slime that hovers somewhere between solid and liquid. I like making quicksand. Halloween is brimming with science, and I like it all.

As a kid I would construct elaborate costumes. Each seemed to teach me a new concept. Once I was a tightly wound mummy that left me breathless. After that I realized that your ribcage needs to expand when you breathe to allow air into your body.

Another year I was a bag of jelly beans. That was bad if you were at all hydrated, because you can't go to the bathroom without releasing your beans.

I've been a vampire—mastering the art of concocting fake blood. I've been a ghost—experimenting with luminosity and transparency.

And I've been a slew of bad puns. When I was in art school, costumes took a more architectural turn. For one party I learned about construction and made a giant column out of chicken wire covered with papier-mâché. I used newspaper headlines as vertical lines to indicate fluting around the column. I was a *newspaper column*! HA! It was a lovely thing. I cut out a hole where I could greet people and chat. If people came close enough I could tell secret tidbits about folks and then claim to be a *gossip column*! It was brilliant.

My heart soared on Halloween, even if I *was* the only one in my family. One year Keith and I were invited to a costume/birthday party for a friend whose birthday was on Halloween. Keith grumbled, but I think he looked pretty damn cute in his costume. It was subtle and funny. We both wore black and then wound fuzzy yellow boas around our necks, waists, and hips. I made antennae out of yellow and black pipe cleaners and ping-pong balls, and attached them to headbands. I insisted Keith wear a tool belt, and I sported a tiara. We both had wings. He was a worker bee, and I was a queen bee.

When we arrived, Keith's antennae bobbed ridiculously; but I didn't tell him how cute he looked. I didn't have a chance. He looked in the window and then turned his head immediately back to me, making those antennae bob comically over his now very stern face.

The door opened. Our friend greeted us with laughter.

"You look great!"

Keith pointed into the crowd. No one else was dressed up, except one French maid and a Dungeons and Dragons guy who greeted us heartily from the far side of the room. They were very happy someone else came dressed up.

"Didn't I tell you it was costume *optional*?" Laura said.

Again, a stern look and bobbing antennae from my little worker bee.

We have a picture of this evening still on our wall. It was the last time I dressed up for Halloween, before I had kids.

When I had kids, and I was plunged into the category of grown-up, Halloween took a new sheen. I could resurrect the practice of costume creation and electrify the kids' costumes with my ingenuity. We could create goo and gak and quicksand and make balloons that screamed.

When they were little, things were grand! I made a white fleece hoodie for Kai with a red comb on top for his first Halloween. I took bright yellow dish gloves and taped them to Kai's feet. They dangled down absurdly as I strapped him face out in the BabyBjörn and donned a yellow beak and matching red comb. The next year, I dressed Keith up as the crocodile hunter and made Kai into an alligator and tossed him on Keith's shoulders. We won contests. We had admiring gazes and shrieks of laughter. Halloween was still wonderful.

Every year we made gak—neon green gak. We'd let it dribble and stretch, we'd roll it into a ball and bounce it. I would extol the virtues of non-Newtonian fluids, Keith would feign interest, and the kids didn't listen at all—though they loved flinging that gak!

Leo was a peapod his first year. Kai was a chili pepper. The next year, Kai chose to be a leaf. We studied leaves and ended up with an oak leaf as a model. Kai insisted that Leo be an accompanying acorn, with a handmade hat and paper-bag body.

They have been lions and tigers and anatomically correct, glow-in-the-dark skeleton bats. No matter what they have been, or what year it was, their fingertips were tinged with neon green from the annual gak batch and they had quicksand beneath their nails.

Halloween day started with a batch of quicksand. I had the box of cornstarch out and a bowl of water and a plastic-lined spot at the table.

"YAY! Quicksand!" Kai yelled. He remembered! He was four and Leo was two.

We mixed up a batch and the kids played.

"What is this stuff, Mama?"

"It's quicksand! It happens in the real world when sand is all squishy with water. But we can make it with this cornstarch and it acts the same. Stir it slowly, and it's all liquidy. But slap it or manhandle it, and it's all hard."

"It's magic," said Leo.

"Magical science!" said Kai, grabbing a handful and rolling it quickly into a ball, then opening his hand to let it ooze out.

"Mom!"

"Yes, Love."

"If this is quicksand, will it suck things up?"

"Maybe . . . what did you have in mind?"

Kai ran and grabbed his box of animals and brought them back to the table—leaving a nice little cornstarch trail. He pulled out an animal and showed it to Leo who was strapped into his seat, playing with the quicksand.

"Tapir!" Leo said as Kai held up the black-and-white animal.

Kai laughed and dropped it on the quicksand in the bowl.

"Tapir in quicksand!" he began to make sucking sounds and then tapir screaming sounds as it got sucked into the fluid.

One by one he dropped in his jungle animals, forest animals, and desert dwellers. And then fished them out—all with running dialogue.

The next year we did the same. After lunch we made a batch of neon green gak, mixing glue and borax solution to create another fluid that could flow and snap and even bounce. We froze rubber gloves filled with red water to put in the punch for later that night.

"Mom, water is like quicksand, isn't it?"

"How so?"

"Well it pours like a liquid, but when we put it in the cold freezer it gets hard."

"That's right. It's called phases of matter. Water can do three phases. Watch."

I turned on the faucet. "Water is a liquid. And when we freeze it it's a solid."

"What's the third one?"

"Gas."

"Gas? Ha ha!"

"Funny. Look. When we take an ice cube and throw it in a hot frying pan, what will happen?"

I tossed a cube into a pan and turned on the heat.

"You have cooked ice."

"Yup. Watch." It seemed like such a cool way to show Kai the phases of matter, but it took too long and he was off. When it did start boiling I called him.

"Kai, come check it out—the ice has melted into water and it's boiling and the steam is the gas. It's all three phases at once."

Kai came around the corner, looked, smiled, and said, "Hunh. Cool. OK, bye!" Then he ran off to get his costume on.

Science is cool, but you can't force it.

That year I outdid myself on the costume front, if I do say so myself. Kai was a Jedi knight and Leo was R2-D2. Keith was Darth Vader and I was Princess Leia. I made the costumes out of cardboard boxes and trash cans with straps and glitter. They lit up and blinked. The paint was metallic. People stopped us in our tracks. We could barely get down the street. Everyone we passed shouted, "R2-D2! JEDI KNIGHT! AWESOME!"

Those were my tricks of the trade, and the compliments, my treats. I collected them in my little bag of self-esteem. It was wonderful. Except it was awful.

The boys hated it. Leo couldn't move. He couldn't get his green-tinged little hands up and out of R2-D2's head. Kai liked Leo's costume better than his own, but couldn't fit in it. They complained the whole evening, begging to be released from their Halloween prison. I smiled at passersby and whispered thickly to Kai and Leo, "But you look so *cute!*"

It was raining, and the cardboard began to tear. The shiny surfaces dissolved into puddles of metallic paste. We went home when their moans hit a high wail. So much for solids and liquids. We melted in more ways than one.

The year they were seven and nine years old, I decided that they could be whatever they wanted, with no input at all from me. They jumped at the freedom.

"I want to be a soldier," said Leo.

"And I want to be a ninja," added Kai. "But we want it store-bought, Mom. *Not* homemade"

The knife! And no mention of quicksand or gak or dry ice or fake blood. Was it over?

"Yeah," chimed in Leo. They clearly had talked about this and were waging a campaign.

The twist of the knife. Store-bought, cheesy nylon costumes that will be lucky to last the evening.

Costumes like everyone else's—no creativity. No pun. Nothing special.

"Are you sure, guys?" I pleaded. "I made an *awesome* dog costume for me and I thought you guys could be fleas or a fire hydrant."

"NO!" they both yelled.

"OK. We could do a soldier and a ninja with cool handmade cardboard armor—"

"Please Mom, please, please, please, *please* can we just be like everyone *else* this year?"

I relented.

I felt the quicksand turn from solid to liquid and pour through my fingers. I felt the gak ooze away and the ice-cube hand melt into a puddle. Things were changing and I couldn't hold on. I had to let go.

That afternoon I took them to town and we went into one of those Halloween stores that pop up in September and disappear November first. They remind me of the umbrella sellers that appear out of nowhere in New York City as soon as it starts to drizzle and then evaporate once the sun comes out.

These places are scary. They are filled with screaming skulls, zombie babies, and all amounts of gore and shock. They are very disturbing places—yet compelling in some ways. I find I could always use a purple wig and a kit to vampirify—you never know. Off the main room with all the creepy stuff are the kid rooms with racks of cheaply made costumes. The kids were in heaven.

They danced in excitement. They carefully inspected every single costume at least five times before finally deciding on the exact right soldier and ninja. They bubbled with happiness all the way to the car and immediately unwrapped their costumes.

I still loved my dog/flea/fire hydrant idea. I silently stewed.

"Mom, can we have drive-through dinner chicken nuggets?" asked Leo in his army helmet.

"Please, please, please, please?" they both chimed.

I was powerless.

"OK, OK," I said. I toyed with the idea of telling them how those things were made and how excruciatingly icky the pink goo was before being fried to a gummy, solid nugget, but I realized it was too scary even for Halloween time, and they should be able to delight in these things. Lord knows that growing up, we all had worse—and loved it.

"YES!" they sang.

"This is the BEST DAY OF MY LIFE!" shouted Leo.

"ME TOO! BEST DAY EVER!" yelled Kai.

The best day of your life? The best day? Out of all the days so far, this tops the cake? I mean, limit it to only Halloweens, and I'm still reeling. For crying out loud, I fashioned an R2-D2 out of a kitchen garbage can for you; sewed on fleece combs and chicken legs; made leaves, acorns, alligators, tigers from scratch. You were transformed into a shining knight by cardboard and spray paint . . . and LOVE! Not to mention the concoctions, the quicksand, the gak!

Then there was the matter of the food! Every year I painstakingly make mozzarella cheese and green olive "eyeballs," pizza dough and almond fingers, and pudding in a brain mold! All it took was a polyester costume and bad chicken nuggets for the best day . . . ever?

In that moment of colossal self-pity and woundedness, I realized something. Something important. I had to grow up, wear the cloak of adulthood, and pass the Halloween wand to the kids. I had to reboot my hard drive, and instead of doing what I wanted them to want, do what they would savor and remember.

I had to release my grip on the metaphorical quicksand and let it trickle along its own path. I had to face my demons. Retire my cardboard and spray paint. Hang up the gak and realize that I was on my own this year—as a dog.

Woof.

Buying polyester costumes and eating chicken nuggets didn't mean I was a *bad* mom. It meant I was trying even harder than was comfortable to be better. Was I solid? Was I fluid? Or both? I had to re-experiment to find a new result.

I had to learn new tricks. *Not bad for an old dog*, I thought to myself as I ordered chicken nuggets for three at the drive-through.

As we drove off, Leo, between mouthfuls of chicken nuggets, said, "Mom! When we get home, can we put on our costumes and then make gak?"

"Gak! YES!" said Kai. "Mom, I love your gak!"

"And quicksand," added Leo.

"And melty hands and cheese eyeballs . . ."

"And bloody-finger pizza . . ."

Music to this mommy's ears!

QUIRKY QUICKSAND

Quicksand is a soupy mix of water and sand. In the movies it sucks up unsuspecting victims. When it comes to science, quicksand is a substance that acts like a liquid and a solid at the same time. Try this cool quicksand.

WHAT YOU NEED

- 16 ounce box of cornstarch
- Large mixing bowl
- $1/2$ cup water (plus more if needed)
- Food coloring (optional)
- Cookie sheet for playing
- Spoon
- Big Ziploc baggie
- Plastic trash bag (to protect the counter, table, or floor)

WHAT YOU DO

1. Put the cornstarch into the bowl.
2. Slowly pour in the water while mixing with a spoon. Keep pouring until the mixture feels like yogurt or honey.
3. Add a drop of food coloring, if you like, and stir it in.
4. Now sink your hands into your quicksand. Move your hand around slowly and then quickly. Notice a difference?
5. What happens if you slap the surface with your hand?
6. Pour it into the tray and play. Roll it into a ball, and then let it dissolve.

7. Have fun. When you're done, don't wash it down the drain. It will clog. Pour it into the baggie and toss it out when you're finished playing with it.

WHAT'S GOING ON?

This quicksand works like a liquid sometimes because it flows. It also acts like a solid because it can be hard. This is because it is a suspension. The cornstarch molecules are suspended in the water. When you move something slowly through them or pour the fluid, the molecules slide past each other smoothly. When you move too quickly or slap the surface, the molecules line up and grip on to each other acting like a solid. Technically it's called a "non-Newtonian fluid." Why?

Newton noticed that fluids move predictably based on their thickness or viscosity. Temperature changed the flow in an expected way. Cold honey flows more slowly than warm honey. But this cornstarch fluid doesn't behave predictably. The viscosity of this fluid changes with pressure, not temperature. Weird and cool. So if you ever do get trapped in quicksand, move slowly, swim gently, and you will escape. Move quickly or panic, and you'll be history.

⚡ SCREAMING GHOST BALLOON

Vibrating the walls of the balloon really makes this ghost sing!

WHAT YOU NEED

- Balloon
- Hex nut
- Black marker

WHAT YOU DO

1. Squeeze the hex nut through the mouth of the balloon. Make sure that the hex nut goes all the way into the balloon so that there is no danger of it being sucked out while blowing up the balloon.

2. Blow up the balloon, but be careful not to overinflate it, as it will easily burst. Tie off the balloon.
3. Draw a ghost face on your balloon.
4. Grip the balloon at the stem end as you would a bowling ball. The neck of the balloon will be in your palm and your fingers and thumb will extend down the sides of the balloon.
5. While holding the balloon, palm down, swirl it in a circular motion. The hex nut may bounce around at first, but it will soon begin to roll around the inside of the balloon. What is that sound? Could the balloon be screaming? The sound every parent loves . . .
6. Once the hex nut begins to spin, use your other hand to stabilize the balloon. Your hex nut should continue to spin for 10 seconds or more.

WHAT'S GOING ON?

What happens when you change the size of the balloon or the size of the hex nut? Try using a marble instead of a hex nut. Does the marble make the balloon "scream"? Experiment with other objects whose edges may vibrate against the balloon.

This is actually a two-for-one experiment—you're learning about the science of motion and sound. The hex nut circles inside the balloon due to *centripetal* force. Centripetal force is the inward force on a body that causes it to move in a circular path. It is a "center-seeking" force. A hex nut has six sides, and these flat edges cause the hex nut to bounce or vibrate inside the balloon. The screaming sound is made by the sides of the hex nut vibrating against the inside wall of the balloon.

= GAK =

Is it solid or liquid? This goopy stuff is so fun to make and play with.

WHAT YOU NEED

- 4 ounce bottle of school glue (clear glue makes clear gak; and white glue makes non-see-through [opaque] gak)
- 1 cup water

- 3 drops neon green food coloring
- Bowl for mixing
- Chopstick or spoon for mixing
- ½ cup hot water
- Borax

What You Do

1. Make the glue solution. Mix together the bottle of glue, water, and food coloring.
2. Make the borax solution. Take the hot water and stir in borax until it stops dissolving.
3. Make the gak by adding ⅓ cup of the borax solution to 1 cup of the glue solution.
4. When you aren't using your gak, keep it in a sealed plastic bag so it won't dry out. It will stay moist and disgusting for a couple of weeks if you store the bag in the refrigerator.

WHAT'S GOING ON?

When you mix the glue and the borax, a chemical change occurs in the glue, making the glue stick to you less and to itself more. The molecules are not fixed in place, so you can stretch it.

FAKE BLOOD

This fake blood is awesome and tasty. All you need is something to make it thick and colorful.

What You Need

- Tropical fruit punch (Hawaiian Fruit Punch works great)
- 1 cup corn syrup
- 2 tablespoons red food coloring
- 1 tablespoon chocolate syrup
- 2 tablespoons cornstarch
- 1 tablespoon powdered cocoa

What You Do

1. Combine all of the ingredients in the blender and mix for 10 seconds. Since different brands of fruit punch vary in color, you'll need to use your vast experience in making fake blood to tweak the recipe to arrive at your perfect batch of fake blood.

WHAT'S GOING ON?

Each ingredient has a different reason for being in the recipe. Experiment with each element and make your own perfect concoction.

- Corn syrup thickens the liquid.
- Cornstarch makes the liquid less transparent.
- Chocolate syrup and cocoa darken the blood, turning it reddish brown.

19

MEMORY ARCHITECT

WHEN I WAS PREGNANT with Kai it began. I took a ride on the "mommy brain" roller coaster in all its fuzziness, weepiness, and jubilance. What I didn't know at the time was that there is scientific evidence that pregnancy truly changes your brain. Flurries of cells from the forming baby float through the placenta and lodge quietly into the mother's brain—where they remain for *years*! These cells affect brain areas associated with emotion and memory.

What I did know was that my new "mommy brain" drove me to do things for which I now have a perennial commitment. Holiday things. Christmas things. Warm, fuzzy, oh-how-cute things. How did this happen? Is this how traditions are built?

For instance, when the predatory holiday catalogs rolled in that first year, I had no idea how they would change me. I thought that a wooden box advent calendar I found on page 26 of the L.L. Bean holiday catalogue was *the* most darling thing I'd ever seen. Oh how *fabulous* to have a tiny treat for the kids every day leading up to the holiday. But WAIT! Even better than chocolate or treats, *I* could write notes—notes of gratitude and thoughts in keeping with the spirit of the season. But WAIT! Even better—the notes could be clues that lead the kids through the house, yard, and beyond to discover the wonders of family, nature, adventure, the world, and the spirit of the season.

I took my job seriously—I was the *architect* of memories. Everything twinkled with fairy dust and shimmered with the blush of love (you know, or hormones, however you want to see it).

Kai wasn't even walking when I purchased the box online. It was far more expensive than I would normally pay for something, but I told myself to think of the lifetime of happy memories it would provide. Pushing the button to buy was easy!

Ahh. I basked in the radiance of what was to come.

The first year, I wrote elaborate clues and sent us on amazing journeys. "It's December 4—let's go find a dinosaur!" I'd fold Kai into the BabyBjörn and cart him out to the Natural History Museum and we'd mingle with a stegosaurus, an elasmosaur, and a 140-million-year-old allosaurus. We went to find specific images hidden on the third floor of the art museum in a painting by Jacob Lawrence. We discovered the difference between three bear species at the zoo. We saw an African Drumming exhibit, toured the fire station, walked in the woods, made paintings with marbles dipped in paint and rolled them around the inside lid of a packing box. We baked. I wore an apron for the first time in my life! I confess, a *few* adventures were aimed at me—we'd walk to buy an eggnog latte or splurge on a bottle of wine over $10. I was on Christmas fire! I was unstoppable!

In the end, I was *exhausted*. At the end of the season, I gladly packed the hideous advent box away; but the very next Christmas I unearthed it, along with all those other happy ornaments and glittery delights that bedeck the season. Like forgetting the pain of childbirth, I was thrilled to see it and remember my job as memory architect— designer of traditions that would warm the very toes of my kids when they were adults with kids of their own. They'd remember over cinnamon buns and steaming cups of strong coffee, "Oh! Remember how Mom made the holidays sing?"

The next year, Kai was newly aware of snow. The advent calendar notes that year had a snowy slant. We had a lot of fun making snowflakes. The weather cooperated, and we went outside with small squares of black velvet that I had on hand to collect snowflakes and hold them momentarily—long enough for us to have a good look at their fleeting beauty. We looked at them with magnifying glasses and talked about how each flake was different. We discussed the snowy facts: each flake was a crystal. Each flake had six sides. Count 'em! Back in the kitchen, we *made* sugar and salt crystals. We counted to six endlessly! The counter was a lab of potions and dripping experiments.

Somewhere between making up new adventures and creating tiny little six-sided, hand-sewn ornaments and felt placemats, I had the great idea of making a snowstorm for Christmas.

On Christmas Eve, Kai was tucked in bed. Downstairs, Keith and I celebrated with friends and family. Warmth and laughter bubbled around us. Always the queen of the multitask, I refreshed appetizers, filled glasses, and joined in spirited conversation. It would have been so easy to drop the idea of the snowstorm and just *not* do another thing.

But . . . it could be *so cool*!

While the party percolated, I chatted, laughed, and toasted from my place on the floor. With the coffee table as my work surface, I clipped and cut over fifty paper flakes the likes of which had never flurried from anyone before. No two were alike! I meant business. The architect in me was bubbling over with holiday cheer.

Hours later, after the Yule log had burned down, and the wassail bowl emptied, and the guests departed, cheeks aglow and bundled into the night, I tidied up, made ready for Santa, and got the tape and thread and the ladder.

Keith tried desperately to make only quiet squeaks as he climbed the alarmingly vocal ladder. I stifled yawns and aches as I handed him flake by flake, each dangling from its own thread. He taped the ends of the string to the ceiling

"Remind me exactly why we're doing this again?" whispers Keith.

I wax poetic. "We *are* the snowflakes, honey."

"We're flaky? I'd maybe go with that . . ." He reaches to tape another flake to the ceiling.

"Seriously. Think about it. I know it's sappy, but this whole parenting journey we're on is not unlike how snowflakes are born."

"Uh oh, here we go." He climbs down and hugs me tight. "Talk geeky to me, Mama."

We shift to a different area of the ceiling to populate with snow. "These fragile and beautiful flakes start out up there in the clouds. A lone dust speck from who-knows-where floats around and meets up with a water droplet."

"Am I the dust or the drip?"

"Conditions have to be just right. It freezes and forms a six-sided prism. Always six sides."

"Is it always six?" he asks.

"Ha! I knew this would interest you! Yes, six is the magic number. It has to do with how the molecules line up when they freeze. Always a six-sided crystal."

"So there are some rules?"

"It's science, Honey. There are rules, and then there are riffs on the rules. That's the beauty of it."

"OK, so then what happens?" He's back on the ladder, motioning for more flakes.

"The droplet is buffeted in the cloud and bounced around. It warms and cools and changes at each step along the way. It responds by flattening, branching, bonding, and growing in its very own unique style at dizzying heights. Here's the amazing thing. During this part, no two flakes shape themselves in the same way. Then it gets heavy—"

"It *is* heavy."

"Too heavy for the cloud and floats down among billions of others—all different. A mind-boggling array of shapes."

Keith steps down and we both look up. The flakes hung from various and artistically placed heights. It was beautiful. He put his arms around me and we kissed in the paper snowstorm.

"I've always wanted to make out in a blizzard."

"Merry Christmas, Love. Here's to branching, growing, and bonding. And flaking!"

Kai woke the next morning and was giddy. It was the best thing about Christmas. Everything about it warmed my heart. That magic and surprise was the high point. That something handmade and created by us was the most delightful thing to Kai. Sure, there was the ride-on scooter; but after he got tired of zooming around the house, he would always look up and say softly—as if to himself—"snow!" We had done it—and it left me only mildly comatose.

There have been quite a few Christmases since then, and our Leo has joined us. Each holiday has its new polish and tarnish. There was the time I wrapped all the Christmas books and put them in a basket by the tree. Each one to be opened up and read at night on the days leading up to the big day. *Where did I get this stuff?* I wrapped twenty-five extra packages, *and* when we unwrapped, I wanted to be green, so we unwrapped to reuse. I was annoying myself.

What I didn't yet grasp was that I had signed up for a lifetime. Being the architect of memories or the builder of traditions is not a one-time deal. It takes fortitude. Even in the face of being so busy you can't imagine making fifty different snowflakes—even when the boys take turns leaping up to whack the flakes down in February.

"Those are hand-cut!"

"Thought SANTA made them, Mom!" Kai said with a twinkle. Leo's looking at me, wide-eyed.

"Well, think of the *work* he put in . . ."

Every year the advent box stares at me with empty drawers. Another thing I haven't done yet. Maybe I can slip it away? The boys clamber to that advent calendar box every day in December and chide us when the drawers aren't yet filled.

Christmas Eve is the same every year. As we tuck them into bed, clad in their new Christmas Eve PJs, they both look straight at me.

"It's going to snow tonight, right?"

"We'll have to see."

"No two flakes alike, right?"

"Yes, Love."

"Each one with six sides—just like a real crystal, right?"

They do listen! Darn 'em!

I think if I asked them what they got for Christmas last year or the year before they wouldn't have a clue; but they remember the snow. They'll keep my time and energy. That's the magic. Long after the hormones have waged another tide, the snow will stick.

I flash ahead, past the long, happy night ahead of me with scissors and thread and friends and glasses of wine and Keith on the ladder. And I look past more long happy nights in the future to when these little boys, still impossibly small in their beds, have their own families. Maybe we'll all be cutting out snowflakes over glasses of red wine on Christmas Eve. Creating the yearly snowstorm—all of us architects—building traditions for their kids one unique, six-sided flake at a time.

COLLECT SNOWFLAKES

When the snow starts falling, grab your kids, coats and boots, a couple of pieces of black construction paper, and a magnifying glass or two if you have them. As the snow is falling around you, catch a couple of snowflakes on your black construction paper and observe them with your magnifying glass, comparing how the snowflakes are similar and different. Count how many sides or points the snowflakes have and if any snowflakes appear to match.

PRESERVE SNOWFLAKES

If you happen to have a microscope and microscope slides, try preserving snowflakes. All you really need for this activity are the slides, but using a microscope is a fun bonus. Prepare in advance by placing a couple of slides in the freezer so that they won't melt the snowflakes. You will also need hairspray or artists' fixative. Keep these items in a cold area like your refrigerator or an unheated garage.

When it is time to collect and preserve snowflakes, bring out the slides, the hairspray, and a couple of toothpicks. Spray one side of the slides with the hairspray. Catch the snowflakes on the sticky side of the microscope slides, using a toothpick to gently move the snowflake to center it, if needed. Place the slide with the snowflake in a cold area where no more snowflakes will fall on it, such as inside a covered box or in the unheated garage. Leave the slide untouched for several hours so that the hairspray can dry and the water in the snowflake will disappear. You now have the imprint of a snowflake on a slide you can study with the naked eye or a microscope.

MAKE BORAX SNOWFLAKES

If you do not have snow where you live, no problem. Just make your own borax snowflakes. This activity takes about thirty minutes of active preparation and then overnight to grow.

WHAT YOU NEED

- Wide-mouth jar
- 3 pipe cleaners
- String
- Scissors
- A pencil
- Water
- 1-cup measuring cup
- Tablespoon
- Borax (look for it in the laundry detergent aisle at the store)
- Food coloring (optional)
- Ribbon (optional)

WHAT YOU DO

1. Make the flake base. Twist together three pipe cleaners in the center to make a six-pointed star. Use scissors to trim down the ends of the pipe cleaners so they are all approximately the same length and can fit in the jar.
2. Tie a piece of string to one end of the star. Connect the string to the next point by twisting it around the pipe cleaner. Continue around until you connect all the points together with the string, making a snowflake skeleton.
3. Tie another piece of string to one of the pipe cleaner points, and tie the other end around the pencil. Place the snowflake in the jar with

the pencil resting across the mouth of the jar to make sure that the snowflake hangs without touching any part of the jar. Take the snowflake out of the jar.

4. Make the solution. Measure out how many cups of water are needed to fill the jar. Use a teakettle or microwave to boil the water. For every cup of water placed in the jar, mix in three tablespoons of borax. This will make a saturated borax solution. Stir the borax solution with a spoon until as much of it dissolves as possible.

5. Create the crystal. Hang your snowflake in the jar so it is completely covered in the solution. Let it sit overnight. Gently remove your now crystal-covered snowflake in the morning and let it dry by hanging it in a dry jar.

KEEP GOING

- To make colored snowflakes, use colored pipe cleaners and add 1 or 2 drops of food coloring in Step 4.
- To make your snowflakes glow in the dark, paint the pipe cleaner snowflake with glow-in-the-dark paint in Step 2. Let it dry completely before going on to Step 3.
- Tie a ribbon to one point of your snowflake to make a Christmas tree ornament!

AWESOME SIX-SIDED PAPER SNOWFLAKES

Everyone knows how to make paper snowflakes, right? But most people make flakes with four or eight sides. Since real snowflakes always form six-sided flakes, here is a step-by-step guide to folding the paper so you get six points every time.

WHAT YOU NEED

- Scissors
- White copy paper 8½ x 11"

What You Do

1. Start with a square piece of paper. (I used copy paper. To make a square from a standard sheet of copy paper, fold one side down to make a triangle and cut off the excess strip.)
2. Fold the square diagonally to make a triangle.
3. Fold the triangle in half to make a smaller triangle.
4. Fold the triangle in thirds (see illustration).
5. Cut off the top off at an angle (see illustration).
6. Cut shapes from the sides of the triangles.
7. Unfold the paper gently.

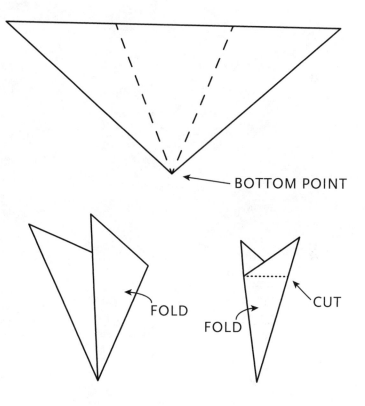

20

IS SANTA REAL?

As PARENTS, if you choose to go down the Santa road, there is the inevitable question that looms like a snow cloud in an otherwise azure sky. What *do* you do when they ask: Is Santa *really* real?

What is *real*, anyway? Our entire perception of our lives is based on brain chemistry and electricity: neurons, electric pathways, serotonin, and synapses. Tweak things just a little, and "reality" becomes something very different. Frankly, I was seriously unprepared when Kai finally asked the big question.

From the beginning, it had been my big idea to make it a family tradition to go into Seattle and see Santa at the top of the Space Needle. Why not? They had a craft area, and a coffee bar. It was sciencey—sort of. It's fun to ride the elevator, and the gift shop sells rockets, robots, and old-fashioned atoms all covered with glitter as Christmas ornaments. I am a sucker for it all.

Traditionally, the Santa there is genuinely Santa-looking. His beard is real, and he's jovial. When Kai and Leo were three and five, it had been perfect. Well, almost perfect. Unfortunately, Kai had thrown up in the car on the way. We cleaned him up as best we could and carried on—we couldn't disappoint him. He sat on Santa's lap, green around the gills and a little stinky, and Leo cried. But that was just *that* year—*that* picture. Santa looked great—even if his smile was a teensy bit strained and he had Kai on the outer edge of his knee.

When Kai and Leo were four and six, it was great. They had made craft foam elf hats and sat enthusiastically on Santa's lap. Leo asked him how he landed on the Space Needle and he quickly replied that his reindeer had sure feet—like mountain goats—and they had no fear of heights. This satisfied Leo. It impressed him enough that he drew reindeer with suction cup feet for years afterward. It also gave us hours of fun in the tub experimenting with suction cups and the unavoidable, fun by-product—suction-cup farting sounds.

When they were five and seven, it was fun. The boys and Santa were old friends now. Santa even remembered them, or at least he seemed to remember them. The craft that year was icing a tree-shaped cookie. Each of my kids did an amazing job defying gravity by piling unspeakable amounts of green frosting and sprinkles on the cookie. That year's picture had Kai and Leo sporting saturated green smiles.

When they were six and eight, things took a turn. We arrived at the Needle, paid our $14, and zipped up the elevator. We listened to the spiel about how it was built for the 1962 World's Fair. When it was built, it was the tallest building west of the Mississippi. It is 605 feet tall—that's 848 steps—and if you happen to use a Milky Way bar for a yardstick, you would have to use 1,320 of them. Kai and Leo were bursting with excitement; but when we arrived at the pinnacle, we were greeted by two space-age elves bedecked in sparkly glitter-red-and-green space suits. That's when we noticed something new: a dual-engine, fiberglass sleighlike spaceship with Styrofoam planets and stars floating on strings around it.

"Wow!" I remarked to the first elf. The color of the "sleigh" was sparkle-plastic-red. It reminded me of my banana-seat bicycle from when I was eight. "Remodel?"

"Yup!" She nodded her head up and down with enthusiasm, emitting a wistful jingle. "This *is* the Space Needle and there's quite a *lot* of *rocket* science going on up here!" She giggled and tickled Leo under his chin.

Rocket science?

Enter Santa. He was dressed in a sparkle-Lycra suit, with three fake fur–coated hula-hoop rings that circled his ample waist and jiggled merrily as he walked. He was like a Santa Saturn.

Was this *our Santa*?

His beard was still real, and he seemed jovial enough as he attempted to wedge his furred hoops into the spaceship to sit down. Eventually with the help of the two space elves and, I think, some duct tape, he was ready to receive. He looked spring-loaded.

Kai and Leo looked on with furrowed brows. They sat on his lap, holding the fur hoops like handlebars.

The picture was taken. Both boys are looking up at Space Santa with disbelief. That was *that* year's photo.

Santa's new, futuristic image was the beginning of the end of innocence for Kai.

Leo was willing to suspend disbelief for a while, as long as Santa made good on a cherry-red Nintendo DS handheld gaming device for Christmas. He has principles.

Kai was pensive. He wanted a DS, too, and he really wanted a bearded lizard (which was *never* going to happen), so he wasn't willing to blow anything; but I could tell. The glitter on Santa's space suit had tarnished something for Kai. I knew he was going to ask, and I struggled to figure out how to handle it.

The moment came five days later, after visiting my mom, who had been recently placed in a nursing home.

My parents had moved from Maine to be nearer to us, and we had some valuable time together before Mom slipped away into the Alzheimer's that was rapidly robbing her from us. I was desperate for her to make some memories with the kids that they could keep well beyond the inevitable. Kai, in particular, had bonded with her, and they had shared many laughs together over cartoons on TV and stories of when I was his age.

Seeing Mom through Kai's eyes was a gift. To him, she was all fun and joy. He wasn't caught up in the pain of losing what she had been. He loved her here and now, the way she was, and so everything made sense.

As Mom disappeared into the gaps, plaques, and tangles of the disease, Science, my old friend, helped me bridge the painful gap between Mom as I knew her and Mom as she was now.

Context plays a role, for sure. What are memories and how are they made? Our memories are an essential part of what makes us who we are. And it turns out a lot of it boils down to chemistry.

There are tiny gaps between nerve cells called synapses. When a memory is made, an electric signal cruises down a nerve cell until it reaches the gap. It can't just jump the gap. But as the signal travels, one cell speaks to another and chemicals are released into the gap. These chemicals allow the signal to leap to the next cell and so on. The more signals that pass along a certain pathway, the bigger the chemical change in the gaps between the cells. If there are only a few signals, the change is temporary and the memory is short-lived. But if the signals keep coming, the chemical changes in the gaps become permanent, forming a long-term memory.

So if you think about something or experience something in a few different ways that are connected, the memories have a greater chance of changing the chemistry of the brain and becoming part of the fabric of your accessible past.

Despite the ravaging biology going on inside Mom's brain, some of the memories remained. Some traditions still garnered a twinkle. Surprisingly, Santa played a part. As my dad became a stranger to her, she would refer to him as "Uncle Santa Claus," with a conspiratorial giggle. While she forgot what a fork was for, she always remembered the melodies and words to her favorite Christmas carols. Mom's Christmas season was extending through the year.

When we had first brought Mom to the home, Kai had visited once or twice; but as she continued down the road she began to not recognize us, and became more and more unpredictable and angry. Dad and I started to visit when Kai was in school, so that he could no longer join us; but he was determined to see her at Christmas.

The year of the Saturn Santa was to be her first Christmas away from us, and we went to the nursing home holiday celebration the week before Christmas. Dad and I girded ourselves in preparation for the holiday "festivities" that awaited: Jell-O, Victorian carolers, fruit punch, grocery store cookies, and a hope that Mom might know us and not be in tears or full of anger.

As we were preparing to leave, Kai, dressed in his best, asked if he could come with us. I was torn. I wanted to include him, to not shield him from this grim reality, but I also wanted his memories of my mom to be full of life and light, not sadness.

Kai insisted.

When we arrived another patient, Mabel, saw Kai dressed smartly in his sweater vest and ambushed him. She wrapped her arms around him and pulled him in close for a long, deep hug. His eyes were wide, peering out between her ample bosom and her tight grip. She began singing to him and rocking back and forth.

I was sure he'd recoil, but he seemed to know what that lady needed. She began to weep for joy, and Kai, instead of pushing away, slowly and carefully reached as far around her as he could and hugged her back.

My father and I stood and watched, speechless. Kai did what I could not have done. The simple act of hugging her allowed the woman to enter a reality in her own head—a place of sheer happiness.

What was that? Was it chemical? I had recently read about how hugs can release oxytocin—a feel-good brain chemical. Was it simply the release of oxytocin in her brain? Was it psychological—did Kai remind her of her own children, so many years before? Or were neurons firing down a corridor, igniting a very real memory in the path of which Kai was caught?

Truth is, we couldn't know for sure; but the result was joy. It was real. There was no mistaking that.

An attendant eventually came and helped Mabel release Kai, and he walked over to me. I hugged him. Poor thing—I hugged him hard, releasing my own oxytocin and choking back my own tears.

"What is it with you making all the ladies cry?"

"Ha ha, Mom."

I whispered into his hair. "You just gave her a great moment, Love. Thank you."

He shrugged and gave a smile. He had been uncomfortable. I mean, it was a weird place to find yourself in; but he rolled with it.

Then we went over to where Mom was seated. She recognized Kai right away, though it had been months. He sat the whole time next to her, holding her hand. Christmas carols played and staff members sang. Patients either sang or stared into space. Mom would sometimes sing a word or two, then fizzle and stare out into the room vacantly. Kai put his face in front of hers every once in a while and said, "Hi Gaga!" and she'd smile. Back for an instant. He'd gently brush her hair away from her forehead, or rub her hand. Anchoring her.

He was so much more able than I was to make this situation less agonizing, and he surprised me by his empathy and warmth. I could barely make it through the carols.

Then Santa came. His big, loud entrance was met the same way the carols were. Some patients noticed. Most did not. Caretakers all around the room enthused loudly, as if to draw out their loved ones. Dad and I did, too; we were grasping for fleeting moments of recognition or happiness that might skate across Mom's face, bringing her sweet flashes of delight.

This Santa's beard was not real at all. The suit didn't even fit him. He didn't look the part. He was dark-haired underneath the ill-fitting beard, which was losing its elasticity. He was warm in the suit, or nervous, because he looked damp and sweaty; but he laughed and gave out gifts of fuzzy socks and dolls and cookies.

Mom delighted in this Santa. She hollered, "HELLO SANTA!" in a loud, clear voice that stunned us all. He came over to her and bestowed a gift of pink socks with rubber treads. He called her by name, and she laughed until she cried. Kai was riveted by the imposter, and never once let go of my mom's hand.

As Santa became more suspect for Kai, he became more real for Mom.

On the ride home, I asked if he had anything he wanted to ask me.

"Mom, is Gaga's brain broken?"

Wow. I had been expecting a question of Santa. This question made me cry.

"Are you OK, Mom?"

"Sorry Sweetie. She's my mom, and it's so hard to see her like that, isn't it?"

"Does everyone's brain wear out?"

"Nope. No one knows exactly why some people get the disease Gaga has. Lots of folks have it. It's called Alzheimer's."

"What does that mean?"

"I think it's someone's name."

"So, why is hers wearing out?"

How do you answer the unanswerable? Taking the scientific approach to discussing Mom's disease had helped me process the fact that I was losing her. It helped me to accept this new reality, no matter how painful it was to let go of the reality I wanted.

"People are kind of like cars. We're made up of different parts, and as we go through our lives we put quite a lot of wear and tear on all our parts. And like cars, sometimes different parts wear out. Sometimes it can be a heart that becomes exhausted from beating too hard. Sometimes it can be a liver that wears out from filtering all the yucky stuff out of our blood. And with Gaga, her brain is wearing out."

"Is yours going to wear out?"

My greatest fear. "Not any time soon, Love."

"How do brains wear out?"

"OK, so your brain is in your skull, right? About the size of a couple of fists. It's made up of these cells called neurons. We have miles and miles of them. They twist and turn all through the brain and allow us to do things like breathe, talk, run, play, sing, remember, eat—everything."

"Eat everything?"

"Very funny, Bugs Bunny. But in a way, they do. They help us figure out what to eat—and *not* to eat everything, because that would kill us."

"How do they do that?"

"Neurons are like roads. Like a huge highway. And little sparks of electricity zip along the roads and trigger different chemicals. Our brain processes these chemicals and electricity as different stuff— like the sound of your voice, or the sound of songs, or of how a candy cane tastes, or how your mom's face looks. And we store these sounds, tastes, and looks as memories."

"So Gaga's neurons don't work?"

"Yeah. They used to work without a hitch, but now she's got a bunch of sticky roadblocks that stop the sparks and the chemicals, so they can't go where they want to and she can't get to some of these stored memories."

"I think the memories are all in there still, don't you?"

"Maybe."

"But she just can't get to them?"

"She can't."

"It's weird."

"I know."

"No, Mom, it's weird that she still thinks Santa is real. Santa's *not* real, is he?"

It *was* about Santa!

"I mean, that guy was *totally* fake!" Kai punctuated the word *fake* with a couple of fist slams into the car seat.

I paused, breathed, and launched into uncharted territory.

"Here's the thing, Bud. I never believed that Santa was *really* a chubby guy creeping into people's houses by going down chimneys. It never made sense. The timing. Time zones. Population of the world. Toys and shipping. Didn't make sense. It doesn't, does it?"

"No . . . I know, but . . ."

I could not stop. It was as if I had just consumed a pot of coffee. "I mean, let's look at this scientifically. How many homes are there with good kids in them? Let's just say, for argument's sake, there are about 90 million. Now how much time does Santa really have?"

"Twenty-four hours?"

"More, if you think about the different time zones and the rotation of the earth, assuming he travels east to west (which makes sense). This gives him probably thirty-one hours."

"OK, Mom . . ."

"With 90 million houses this works out roughly to about eight hundred visits per second. Possible?"

"Probably not . . ."

"So Santa's sleigh would be moving at 650 miles per second, three thousand times the speed of sound."

"Fast?"

"Super fast, Honey. I'm guessing a reindeer can run maybe twenty miles per hour. We can look that up."

"I get your point."

"But, having said all of that, I still *believe* in Santa—in a way."

"What? What does that mean?"

"I don't think he's a *real* guy. But that doesn't mean his *spirit* isn't real. And it sure doesn't mean that the *power* of Santa isn't real."

"I don't get it."

"What does Santa mean to you, to anyone?"

"Goodness, happiness."

"Exactly! And that guy today wasn't *the* Santa but he was *a* Santa, wasn't he?"

"Huh?"

"Well, those people whose brains aren't working so well, he made them happy, didn't he? Even if it was for just a moment. Those people felt *real* happiness."

"Yeah. He gave Gaga socks. She thought he was real."

"Well, he kind of *was* real for her, wasn't he?"

"I guess, but he was so fake!"

"But not for her. Or for the other people, right?"

"He gave that lady who hugged me a doll. She loved it. Then she dropped it."

"Right, but it wasn't the socks or the doll, was it? It was that for a few moments that guy was Santa to them, because he's *like* Santa."

Silence from the backseat.

I continued. "And I have to say how proud I am of you. You were *wonderful* with Gaga. *You* made her happy in a way that no one else could."

"I love her," he said softly. "Even if her brain is broken."

"I know you do, Sweetie. And you holding her hand is like being a Santa."

"But I didn't give her anything and I don't have a beard."

"You were giving her gifts the whole time, Sweetie. Your hugs and your holding her hand and your brushing her hair all stimulated good things in her brain because you touched her."

"That's weird. Me? Santa?"

"OK." An idea was taking shape. I was going with it.

"Now that you're old enough to know . . . you're kind of in the club. You get to *be* a Santa. We all do! You can do quiet things to help people and be kind and make a difference. We get to keep the spirit of Santa and the whole season alive."

"Like hugging that scary lady?"

"Yes. You made her so happy."

"Yeah. But where do the presents come from? And the stockings? Is it you and Dad?"

"What do you think?"

"I think it's you and Dad."

"OK it is, but we're just being Santa. Now you know. When kids are small, the magic of Santa is real. When you're older, that magic just shifts. Now you get to help *make* that magic real. You get to make Santa live. Let's keep him alive for Leo a little while longer. Let's keep him alive for all of us."

"OK, maybe I can climb on the roof on Christmas eve and make hoof sounds and Dad can come too and yell HOHOHO and keep him alive for Leo . . . and maybe we can drop some black olives in the snow by some hoof prints and it could be reindeer poop!"

"Inspired ideas, Bud, but I think for right now—just don't tell him yet. He's not old enough to know the magic secret. You're old enough. Now you have the power to make someone happy."

"Just by touching them?"

"Kind of."

There was silence in the car as we rolled along past all the lit-up houses and sparkly trees on our way home.

"Mom?"

"Yes, Love?"

"Can I have a bearded lizard for Christmas?"

"Uh, no. No bearded lizard. The cats would eat it."

"But, if I can get to *be* a Santa, I wonder if a bearded lizard would just be a wonderful reminder for me—"

"I'll make sure you have enough reminders, Sweetie."

"Well, how about a komodo dragon? They're big. Cats won't eat that."

"Nope. I couldn't handle feeding the thing whole pigs."

"But MOM! Think about making me *happy*! Think about Christmas *magic*!"

"There will be magic, Honey. I promise. It'll just be *different* from now on. And it won't be reptilian, trust me."

That night, after tucking both boys in and reading *The Grinch* for the umpteenth time, I puttered around my office. I found an index card and poked two holes for fingers at the bottom. I made the card dance. It gave me an idea—just a small, sweet one I thought might make a difference to Kai. Something that would ignite a memory and keep the signal traveling along the neurons until the chemistry changed enough to remember this day forever.

I drew my best Santa, decorated it with glitter glue, and cut it out. On the back I put a picture of him and Gaga from that day. Then I put the Santa finger puppet on his bedside table with a note: "Dear Kai, Place fingers here and have fun being Santa."

This most recent Christmastime, one night after the boys had read themselves to sleep, I went into Kai's room and removed the book that had fallen open on his chest. It was *The Grinch Who Stole Christmas*. When I picked it up, the bookmark fell out. It was the old finger puppet. The edges of the Santa were a bit frayed, and the finger holes were wide and worn. Some of the glitter had made its way to the back and clung to the picture of Kai and Gaga.

It sparkled quietly in the darkness.

💡 MULTIPATHWAY MEMORY-MAKING FINGER PUPPET

This finger puppet worked to make an important memory for Kai. For him, that day with my mom will last forever. It's connected with Santa, it's connected with Mom, and it's connected with him. Plus it's interactive, and he can feel it and move it around—each time remembering and making those chemicals in the gaps between his synapses permanent.

WHAT YOU NEED

- An index card or any card stock
- Scissors

- A coin with a diameter as wide as your index finger
- Markers/crayons
- Photographs
- Glitter—anything you have laying around—feathers, sequins, jiggly eyes, glue

What You Do

1. Flip the index card to the unlined side, and put it on the table so the length is vertical—up and down.
2. Using the coin as a template, make two circles about a $\frac{1}{2}$ inch up from the bottom, and cut them out.
3. Place your index and middle finger through the holes. These are the legs of your puppet.
4. Draw the body, and cut it out. Make sure there's at least a $\frac{1}{2}$ inch around the leg holes so your puppet won't lose its legs.
5. Flip it over, and affix a photo or a collage or even words cut out from magazines that you want to remember.
6. Decorate your puppet with markers, glitter, or whatever you like.
7. Stick your fingers through and kick up your heels!

WHAT'S GOING ON?

Keeping photographs in a frame or a book is a common way to remember big events, but it's only one way—a visual way—to stimulate a memory. Amp up a memory by linking in different senses. Make it interactive somehow—add a scent or some glitter (for sparkle and texture), associate it with a song or a quote, make it something to touch as well as see. It can drive a memory into your brain along different pathways and change the chemistry of your brain permanently. Plus, it's fun!

After my beloved Aunt Jo died, we inherited some old family photos. I scanned them, and the kids and I had a blast one year making angel ornaments out of them for our tree and for gifts to family members. Now they remember a great aunt they never met as "that angel Aunt Jo" on the tree. Warms *my* heart every year!

21

ADHD

KAI DIDN'T TAKE TO READING as we had hoped. We thought he was a late bloomer. Perhaps it was immaturity. He was such a bright boy.

When he reached second grade, we noticed that he couldn't sit still. He couldn't keep quiet. He couldn't focus, and he walked on his toes.

It's weird when you start to notice something isn't going as you planned with your kid. You don't want to say the word *wrong*, but you worry. I worried about Kai's behavior for a while, even before anyone pointed it out to me. When the teachers at school did mention something, I was offended and rejected their comments.

"Kai lacks focus" is what they said.

"Bullshit" is what I said. He's a late bloomer. He's not challenged enough. He's overcompensating because he's younger than the rest of the kids. He's immature. He's acting out because he can't read as quickly. I had all the answers.

Truth is, Kai was struggling. It was hard for him. He was acting out. He was not focusing. Immediately, I did what any self-possessed mother would do. I blamed myself. What am I doing wrong? What am

I feeding him? It's that occasional sports drink that I allowed him to have. The molecules that make it orange are what caused this; I just *know* it.

ADHD—Attention Deficit Hyperactivity Disorder—was bandied about in conferences. ADHD! It seemed like such a disorder of the day, like Chronic Fatigue Syndrome or Carpal Tunnel Syndrome—disorders that were as common as pimples on teenagers.

I knew that when it comes to boys in school, ADHD was ubiquitous. At least, the diagnosis was. Boys don't learn the same way girls do. School is presented in one way. Sit still, listen, learn, and tell me what you learned. Boys like Kai need action: physical and kinetic challenges. Some children are spatial or tactile learners; they just need a different approach.

We hired tutors. I devised all sorts of physical games for him. The poor guy bounced on the trampoline endlessly, trying to get spelling words to make sense. I coated the counter in whipped cream, and he drew his spelling words in foam. I came up with songs; he was musical, and I knew that having things come in a tune would help.

It all sort of worked—but not really.

Then our neighbor Rose, a physical therapist, noticed that Kai was walking on his toes. She said I should check it out. Toe walkers are sensory seekers. It's an indication that his brain needed more stimulation. She gave me books. I read all about sensory seekers. It didn't seem to fit what Kai was experiencing. He wasn't the kid that hated the scratchy tags in his shirts, or hated loud music or fireworks.

So we tried yoga and diets and vitamins and exercises that crossed the center line, exercises that exhausted him, exercises that would get the blood flowing. We stretched. We jumped. We concentrated. We saw counselors.

He still couldn't focus.

I approached it in my comfortable, most-persistent-camper, multitasker way. I removed whey from his diet. I took him off dairy. I increased protein. I added vitamin B as a supplement.

He still couldn't focus.

We had him sit on huge balls, chew gum, stretch bungee cords, walk between classes, wear tight shirts, listen to classical music when he read.

He still couldn't focus.

And worse, he was really aware that he was different.

We had him tested for ADHD. We took tests, answered questions, and had his teachers take tests and answer questions about Kai.

Does your child have difficulty sitting still?

Doesn't everyone?

Does your child have a short attention span?

Doesn't everyone?

Does your child move quickly and frequently between tasks?

Doesn't everyone?

It went on like this for pages. The last one caught my eye.

Has anyone else in your family been diagnosed with ADHD?

During this process, I became aware that maybe Kai did have ADHD. I also became aware that I was possibly slightly ADHD myself; but having been it for my whole life, I have nothing to which I could compare myself. It was my normal. It works for me. I like to think of it as extreme multitasking. I have learned to not only cope with it but also thrive with it. Maybe I had handed this genetic cocktail to Kai; and maybe it wouldn't work so well for such a young boy.

Kai was diagnosed with ADHD. The doctor told us it was like the brain was command central. Too many pieces of information were coming in, so it was confusing. The brain needed even *more* to concentrate.

That night, Kai whispered to me in bed. "Mom, *why* do I have to have ADHD?"

"I don't know, Love. It's not wrong or whackadoodle, it's just what it is. It's like you have a super amazing race-car engine for your brain—ready to BLAZE! But you have lawnmower brakes. It's a little imbalanced. We can work with it. We can tinker with the brakes."

"Mom, the doctor called it a *disorder*. I'm not stupid."

"I wouldn't call it that. I think I have this thing, too, Kai. In fact, I probably gave it to you. It's just what we have to deal with. It's just what *is*. You and I don't like really hot showers. We feel pain, we're sensitive. We're also creative and funny and thoughtful. I have found that whatever this thing is, it really *works* for me. We just have to get your race-car engine and your lawnmower brakes in sync. Then you'll blast off! In the meantime, we have work to do. So, you get a little antsy sometimes."

"*Sometimes?* Mom, I can't sit still. I try, but I can't. Everything— the yoga, the food, the music, the bouncing. It doesn't work. I pretend it does sometimes, because I don't want you to be mad."

"Oh, Kai! Why would I be mad?"

"Because I'm not focusing! I can't! I can't do it! You can! You write books and stuff. I *can't* do that!"

"Honey, you forget that I'm ancient! I have had eons to work with this. I've souped-up my lawnmower brakes and found the balance with a lot of work and sweat and, yes, tears. I'm not saying it's easy. But it *is* what it *is* and frankly, there are some really good things about this. But, I know how you feel."

"I don't think you do."

"Oh, Love. I do. You know what? I've never told anyone this, but you know how you walk on your toes?"

"Yeah, it's fun. It's like dancing."

"I get it. I used to rock my head back and forth on my pillow before I went to sleep."

"You did?"

"Yup. It was the only way I could kind of think through the day and unwind."

"That's weird, Mom."

"Thanks, Kai!"

"I'm kidding. Although it is kind of weird."

"When I was young I thought it was weird, too, but I couldn't stop it. If I had sleepovers, I didn't sleep because I didn't want people to make fun of me. So I totally get what you're feeling. But remember. Everyone has something. Some people have no rhythm. Some people can't hit a note to save their lives. Some people don't run fast. Some people are mean. Some people like grapes. Some don't. Everyone has something they have in their bag of tricks to deal with. ADHD is just one of those things. ADHD is what it is. It's not something to fix. It's something to embrace and learn to live with comfortably."

"So I have to just suck it up?"

"Well, no. We're working on some strategies to help you make it work better for you."

At this point, Kai began to sob. "Nothing is working!" he screamed.

I realized I needed to know more about what the heck ADHD *was*. I needed to stop operating solely from *my* perspective.

What I learned was that in the brain of an ADHD person, certain receptors that normally respond to the neurotransmitter called *dopamine* are not working properly. Dopamine is the feel-good chemical that makes us feel satisfied after we eat a great meal, learn something new, or fall in love. It's an important chemical—one that I wanted Kai to have functioning well.

I also learned that ADHD brains had some different structural elements. There are differences in size, structure, and symmetry between the brains of boys with ADHD and boys without. The prefrontal cortex, which is the brain's command center, and the caudate nucleus and the globus pallidus, which translate commands into action, have slight physical differences. Brain scan studies also showed that the ADHD brain may use these areas differently. It appears that boys with ADHD have an increase of activity in two structures: the frontal lobe and striatal areas below it. These areas work in part to control voluntary action. So the ADHD boys work harder to control their impulses than non-ADHD boys.

ADHD is not a willful behavior. It is not brought about by too much TV, too much sugar, or bad parenting. It's simply a difference in the brain—a difference that was causing Kai challenges and preventing him from experiencing things efficiently. If we kept ignoring this, it might blossom into something worse for him.

I looked at studies that showed what happened when this condition was treated with drugs. Certain drugs like Ritalin quieted down the parts of the brain that were in overdrive. Once quieted, the ADHD brain was offered the ability to function more efficiently. Keith and I had been avoiding an avenue that might actually help him because we were ashamed. So embarrassing. Why? I think we didn't want to look like bad parents—bad because we caused the ADHD, and bad because we were copping out and drugging him.

Truth is, it isn't about us! Duh!

We had to deal with our own stigma. Drugs might actually lift the veil for Kai and allow him the freedom to laser into what he was doing. We looked to drugs.

Why is it such a dirty word when it comes to actually helping with a reality? Our perception is dictated by chemicals and electricity. These things are in a fragile balance. Kai's chemicals were off-kilter, and it was getting in his way. Why wouldn't we help him?

We live in the twenty-first century. These drugs are available. Of course we don't want to abuse them, or take him down a path that would hurt him in the end; but if these things could help him, why would we not try them?

Our journey has not been perfect, but it has been working. Kai responded immediately to the drugs and felt stronger and more enabled to direct his own behavior.

There are also side effects. He doesn't want to eat, and he has difficulty sleeping. He also has temper flare-ups—usually because he doesn't want to eat and he is hungry.

Some days he hates the pill that he takes. Other days it's what allows him to climb the mountains. It's a balance beam we walk. Every day is a new step. Sometimes we teeter and wave our arms. Sometimes we fall; but we keep moving forward. We climb back up. We multitask. We tweak the lawnmower brakes. We walk, we juggle, dance, tell stories, and laugh.

Never a dull moment. And I wouldn't want it any other way.

DRIVEN TO DISTRACTION

How well can you do a task when you have no distractions? How well can you do it while listening to music? Listening to a story? Thinking about something else? Try these interesting experiments to get a sense of what it might be like to operate with ADHD.

1. Think about the taste of a perfect strawberry. That burst of sweetness across your tongue. The little seeds that give a tiny crunch. The sweet juice dripping . . . Do it at the exact same time as you

add 27 and 16. At the *same* time. Really try. Can you do it? Probably not. It's impossible. What happens is your brain flips back and forth between tasks super quick, but you simply can't do both at the same time.

2. Try and remember the smell of a fresh mown lawn *and* all of your teacher's names since kindergarten. Then on top of that, try spelling *purple*.

3. Try humming a song and reading this paragraph while tapping your fingers and counting to 100.

4. Time yourself doing the following two actions:
   - Spell aloud, letter by letter, "Strange and Weird" at the same time as you write your mother's full name.
   - Spell aloud, letter by letter, "Strange and Weird" and then, after you are done with that, write your mother's full name.
   - What's the difference in time?
   - Now practice spelling "Strange and Weird" out loud for a few minutes.
   - Try the task again: spell aloud, letter by letter, "Strange and Weird" at the same time as you write your mother's full name.
   - How long did it take you?
   - Chances are since you practiced it you won't have to concentrate as hard on doing it and you will be able to do both tasks faster.

WHAT'S GOING ON?

What does this have to do with ADHD? For someone who functions with this condition, life comes at you from every which way. Doing simple tasks is never simple when you have information bombarding you from every angle.

When I find myself being impatient with Kai I simply remember these exercises and put myself in his shoes. It gives me a fresh perspective.

22

WINE AND DINE

NINE-YEAR-OLD KAI and I took the ferry one early summer evening to Seattle for a Mommy-and-me date. We had decided on Italian, and I knew this cool little hideaway Italian place in Pioneer Square.

He dressed up in a Hawaiian shirt and shorts, and I in a sundress. We were excited for a fun evening. I was looking forward to showing him the finer points of how to treat a date: open doors, please and thank you, don't smack your lips, no running around the restaurant while waiting for the food, no burping loudly . . . you know, classic stuff.

The place was within walking distance of the ferry—although it meant walking through a high-pedestrian-trafficked, small, dicey area notoriously populated with vagrants and addicts.

I had shielded Kai from this part of real life but thought that he was probably ready to see it and be exposed to this life lesson.

The first chance came hard and fast. Immediately when we got off the ferry, we passed a handful of homeless folks with cardboard signs asking for money.

One shaggy guy in particular saw Kai and said, "Hey, kid, do you have any money?"

He had a desperate look in his eye that scared me but hit Kai in a deep spot.

"We do! Mom, can we give him our money?"

The shaggy man looked at me hopefully. He smelled like a brewery. I looked at him and smiled.

"No, not tonight," I said. "Have a good evening."

I felt awful about it.

"Mom, *why* didn't you give him money? He needed it, and we have it."

"Sweetie, I'm not so sure he would spend the money well."

"What do you mean?"

"I think he may have a problem with using drugs or alcohol."

"What does that mean? And what does that have to do with money?"

"Well, Honey, everything. That guy is down on his luck, and quite possibly because of the choices he has made."

"Like what?"

"Like taking drugs or abusing alcohol."

"I don't get it."

Oh my gosh! A drug-and-drinking talk. Age nine. I was *not* expecting the evening to be this; but there you go. Yay Mommy-and-me!

We arrived at Il Napoli and were seated right away. I ordered a glass of red wine for me, and Kai ordered lemonade.

"Mom, you drink wine. If you needed money, I would give it to you."

"That's nice, Honey," I said and swigged my wine.

"Sometimes people drink alcohol because they like how it tastes and how it makes them feel. Others don't stop at just one or two, and need to have more and more to make them feel good. Something happens in their brains. The drinks or the drugs change the pathways in their brains."

"Pathways?"

"Brains are amazing things. They are made up of cells—just like the rest of your body, but these cells are different."

The restaurant had paper table covers, and there was a cup of crayons in the center. I picked up purple and drew a blob.

"Here's a nerve cell—called a neuron. Your brain is loaded with them. Whenever you have a new thought or learn something, you start to make pathways like this."

I drew a branching line with a small gap and then another line to a new neuron.

"The more your reinforce the thought or idea, the stronger the pathway becomes."

I darkened the lines.

"So when you learn what two plus two is, you get a new path?"

"Yup. And when you recognize blue and learn that the opposite color on the color wheel is orange, and when you touch cats and they feel soft, or when you smell what a horse smells like . . . all of these things. New pathways. Brains are so cool."

"OK, but what does this have to do with drinking or drugs or that hairy guy needing money?"

"Well, those things are chemicals. Drugs and alcohol are chemicals that kind of change things in the brain. See these spaces here, between the branchy bits of neurons? Sometimes chemicals can scramble things up here. Sometimes they can make impulses zip across these spaces super fast."

"Is that bad?"

"Not always. The problem is that it can feel really good. These chemicals stimulate the 'reward' part of the brain. But it's a trick. While it might make you feel good, it's actually changing your cells and setting in motion a pattern that 'teaches' people to repeat the behavior of abusing drugs—making some not-so-great pathways very strong. Pathways that tell you that 'I can only be happy if I take this drug.' Or 'I need to drink more and more, no matter what.' When this happens, people do anything to get more. They lose sight of things that matter, like family or friends or jobs. They get lost. Like that guy on the street. Not all addicts end up like that, but some do."

"So if chemicals *make* your brain think that way, how can you say that guy made bad choices? It doesn't sound like he *had* a choice, if it's his brain making the decisions."

"You are so smart. That's what addiction is. You always have the choice to put these chemicals into your body. It's *your* choice to start. To *try* these things. To experiment. But you never know whether or not your brain might actually short-circuit when you do. He probably made the choice to try it awhile back, and it really changed his brain. Now he lives on the street. He begs for money. He doesn't work, and people are scared of him. It's not a great life he has right now, is it?"

"Because he did drugs?"

"Maybe. You know, some of these people that end up on the street also have illnesses. Their brains and the pathways between their neurons work differently. It's hard."

"But we didn't help him."

"I know. We didn't. Giving him money would not have helped him, either. He needs what we can't give him. And truthfully, it makes my heart ache. He's someone's kid. He's grown up and hairy and smelly and scary, but he's still a person and he's someone's baby. It makes me feel terrible, and I don't know what to do to help him. But what I do know is that *we* can look at that situation and *we* can talk about it, and hopefully I can help you become educated and teach you that there are terrible things in this world that you can't fix. But there are some you can prevent. Does that make sense?"

"Not really."

"I mean that we can't fix that guy. But we can still learn from him."

"How?"

"Well, you can understand that maybe his predicament was set in motion by making bad choices. By partying with friends, by maybe sneaking out and drinking or trying drugs. Kids do that. You will know kids who do it. Some of your friends right now will grow up and try these things."

"Will they end up like this guy?"

"Probably not, but you never know. What you can know is that you are in charge of your own choices."

The waitress appeared and asked us if we had decided. The timing was so perfect. I smiled at Kai. He got the joke. It was as if I could see the neuron making a pathway. He smiled as well.

"Spaghetti and meatballs, please," he said.

I ordered the chicken smothered in capers and wild mushrooms. She smiled and left. I took another sip of wine.

"Mom, did you sneak out and drink or try drugs?"

I looked at him.

"Honey, I was a geek. I was not one of the popular kids. I totally wanted to fit in, but I knew too much about what happens to your brain when you do stuff like that, so I was way too scared to even try any drugs. And it was OK. I had some great friends. And as far as drinking? Many of my friends did. I didn't until college. Then I did, and I discovered my boundaries."

"What?"

"I learned that more than two glasses of anything was way too much for me. My body let me know."

"How?"

"Well, I got super dizzy and sick to my stomach."

"You puked?" has asked with delight.

"Yes, Honey, I did; and it taught me that I didn't exactly find that fun, and so it's not a pathway I strengthened."

"Well, I am *never* drinking or doing drugs—ever! And *none* of my friends will, either."

"I like your resolve, but I also know that things might change. As you get older, your friends will become even more important to you. You'll want to fit in and belong. It's normal. It's what happens to everyone. Some of your friends might try and shame you into trying stuff—like booze or drugs. They'll make you feel like you *have* to do it. It's called 'peer pressure,' and it's *really* hard to deal with. Hard, but not impossible. Know that it's coming, and you can be strong. See, we have addiction on both sides of our family. You have it in your genes. It may or may not ever become a problem for you. So when people push you, you can say 'no.' You can say, 'I like dancing too much to scramble my brain.' Or you can say, 'We have addiction in our family, and I don't want to go there.' You will learn that some friends are not friends. And you will *never* get in a car with anyone that has been drinking or doing drugs. You will have a cell phone by then—"

"I will! Awesome!"

The horse. The galloping. It was a familiar urge for me, and I could not stop it.

"You will have a cell phone and you will use it to call me or Dad anytime you feel uncomfortable. You will have my permission to blame me for being a mean mom and not letting you go to parties where there will be booze or drugs—you can use me. I will take one for the team, and we'll have a secret word like *rutabaga* that you can use that lets me know we need to come and get you. We have your back. And we trust you."

"Mom! I get it. Thanks. I'm, like, *nine*. I am not going to these parties!"

"You're right. I know. But I want you to be armed with knowledge."

The meal came. Kai ate his spaghetti with elegance. We chatted about music and street gymnastics and magic tricks. He was so much more sophisticated and cool than I was at his age. He was cooler than I am now!

"You will be invited to parties and friends will try and force you to do stuff you don't want to do. You may even be tempted. Changes are on the way. "

"Oh no, Mom! Not the *magical* journey of adolescence *again*!" he laughed.

"*Always* the magical journey, my love! I will stop after I say this last thing. I promise. Believe it or not, it all starts in the brain, with these pathways. You get more independent. It's kind of like you're in training to be a grown-up. You start to make your own choices, and you hang with your friends. You're making new pathways and you're kind of ditching pathways that don't get used. Build strong pathways—"

"Mom?" he said as he twirled the last few strands of angel hair on his plate.

"Yes, Love?"

"Look, I am making noodle pathways between my meatballs."

"Ha! And what pathways are you strengthening?"

"This meatball is me and that one is you. The spaghetti in between is really strong."

I finished my wine and reached out to hold his hand.

"Stronger than you know, Love."

We finished up. Kai had dessert. I had the leftovers of my dish packed up. We carried it with us back to the boat. When we passed the man with the sign, we stopped. I handed the bag to him.

"Just some leftover chicken and pasta. Sorry it's not more."

He grabbed it, tore it open, and started eating with his hands. He smiled. "I love pasta! Just like Mom used to make."

I took Kai's hand and we walked on to the ferry home.

MAKING PATHWAYS

Your brain is changing every time you learn. New things may seem impossible to learn at first. But after a while and after practice, you can master them. How? As you practice, messages travel over and over along certain pathways of neurons in your brain, making them stronger. Thoughts and memories work this way, too. Here's a cool experiment to try with the kids.

WHAT YOU NEED

- Tray or plate
- 10 to 20 small items (like an eraser, pencil, coin, marble, etc.)
- Cloth or towel to cover the tray
- Timer
- Paper and pencils
- Jump rope

WHAT YOU DO

1. Put 10 to 20 objects on a table or a tray, and cover them with a towel or cloth.
2. Tell the players that you have a number of objects under the cloth. They will have 1 minute to look at the objects. Then the objects will be covered again, and the players will have to write down as many objects as they remember.
3. Take off the cover from the tray, and time for 1 minute. After 1 minute, cover up the tray.
4. Have the players write down all the items that they can remember.
5. Have all the players jump rope or do calisthenics for 5 minutes. While they are exercising, rearrange the items on the table or tray and cover them back up.

6. After the exercising, immediately try the game again. Do you see a difference?

WHAT'S GOING ON?

Exercise makes you feel better and strengthens your body, but scientists have recently learned that for a period of time after you've exercised, your body produces a chemical that makes your brain more receptive to creating new pathways and learning.

Try the exercise trick during homework time. Reinforce those pathways. I have found that a break to bounce or run around or ride a bike allows the blood to flow, and the kids find that work is easier afterward.

23

NEWTON AT THE PLATE

I THINK IT WAS IN FIFTH GRADE when I learned the Isaac Newton gem: "An object in motion stays in motion unless acted upon by an outside force." I don't think I had a clue about what that really meant. I'm sure I did well on the test that talked about balls rolling down a bowling alley and slowing down because of friction and, of course, those pins and the wall behind. I probably answered correctly questions about space ships or satellites that continued in an endless loop in space because there is nothing to act on them or stop them. It was cool. It was science. It made sense. Balls, space ships. Whatever.

I did not know then what I am still learning now: these laws of Newton's are what make the world go around—both literally and metaphorically.

Take baseball, for instance.

We ran smack-dab into these laws of Newton's when Kai and Leo embarked upon that great American tradition of Little League. I have to admit with the coming of spring and the smell of fresh cut grass in the air and that *crack* of the bat against the ball, my heart begins pounding a little faster.

When Kai and Leo were ready for T-ball, I rediscovered an inner ember of warmth for the game I loved as a girl and fanned it.

T-ball was *adorable*! Kids looking up from beneath impossibly large-visored bright hats and oversized team jerseys. They took themselves so seriously one minute, swatting at the ball on the tee; then, in the field, spent time picking flowers and waiting for the team cupcakes and juice boxes after the game. They didn't keep score in T-ball. Every kid swung until they hit. It was all very supportive, and we parents exchanged sweet glances of pride and joy at how we had evolved and how our progeny was so endearing.

We all made new friends. The kids bonded with their teammates, and Keith and I made new friends among the parents—especially when we cheered each other on as our breath hung in clouds and we jiggled our feet amiably to keep circulation going during those dark, early spring, late afternoon games.

It wasn't all idyllic. There were hailstorms and moments of bitter cold as the sun set early in the Pacific Northwest. There were melt-downs and gluten allergies and hurt feelings and sportsmanship chal-lenges to accommodate; but it was still fun. Until the kids got a little older and the game became more serious.

When Kai had graduated into the league where kids were learning to pitch, it sounded promising. He was excited. The practices went well. Kai was enjoying his teammates and getting better at hitting and catching and throwing. The uniforms were good. We hadn't yet met any of the other parents but were looking forward to the games so we could all watch and bond together—just like we had during T-ball.

Then the games started.

The first thing we, as parents, were asked to do was sign a contract promising our good behavior. As I read it, it started to creep into my consciousness to wonder *why* we needed to do this. As a sophisti-cated, educated group of responsible parents, *why* would we need to sign this contract promising things we should already have an inner promise with ourselves to do? The conduct outlined in these contracts consisted of simply decent, kind, and reasonable behaviors—nothing so unusual that we ought to be reminded of it.

Keith and I exchanged looks, laughed it off, and signed our names. We had promised to:

Refrain from insulting the referee and the coaches.

This seems like a fair request. They are just parents in uniform doing their best, right? They are human.

Let coaches do the coaching (and not interfere).

Who would tread into the world of annoying parents and try to coach the coach? Sheesh! Of *course* not us!

Keep from yelling critical remarks to team members.

I remembered my own Little League days and being heckled by a parent for being a girl. This *could* be a useful thing for people to sign. After all, some grown-ups can be jerks.

Put the well-being of the athletes before a personal desire to win.

This makes sense. It is a game. The definition of a game is to have fun, right? Plus the kids are only eight years old.

Treat other parents and athletes with respect.

Well, duh!

Who wouldn't sign this and abide by it, right? I mean it couldn't *really* be a problem. Not on *Bainbridge*, right?

For me, baseball was still about Newton and physics. Each day I picked Kai up from practice and extolled upon the virtues of physics. I shared the logic and science of it with Kai and encouraged him to apply it to every element of the game.

Newton's First Law of Motion: Objects at rest remain at rest unless acted upon by an outside force, and objects in motion remain in motion unless acted upon by an outside force.

Think of a pitcher. The ball is in his glove and is not moving. He throws the ball—puts some force on it—and it flies across the plate. The flying ball is moving. It is stopped by either the bat or the glove of the catcher. Simple. Elegant. Science.

Newton's Second Law of Motion: You can apply the same amount of force on two objects of different mass and there will be a difference.

If you hit a baseball and a bowling ball with a bat, the baseball will no doubt go farther!

Newton's Third Law of Motion: Action and reaction.

A ball is speeding across the plate, and you swing at it. You change the direction of the ball—you will also feel it in your hands as the ball hits the bat.

I was in my element.

Kai sat in the backseat emitting the periodic "huh" and "OK" and "hmm." As the season unfolded, it didn't take me long to realize that, for Kai, baseball *wasn't* about applying science principles. It was still all about the uniform, the team fun, and the freedom to practice dance moves or explore dandelions close-up out in the outfield. He was eight years old. He had to discover his own passion.

Many of the boys were older and really, intensely passionate about winning. On our team, the ones who weren't intense at the beginning began to take on the intensity because of the other players and the coaches. The coaches and the assistant coaches were really enthusiastic.

There were lots of tears shed on days when the team lost. The parents in the stands would ache along with their kids. They would stress over each inning and time up at bat. They would holler "encouragement" and "reminders" for their own player to pay attention, keep an eye on the ball, swing with strength.

Kai was stuck in the outfield game after game because he wasn't as intense about playing. The coaches gave him time in the game, but it was clear they increasingly wanted to *win* games rather than teach kids to play and love the game. Had *they* seen the contract? Had *they* signed it? Keith and I didn't really care. Kai didn't really care. It was becoming clear that, for us, baseball itself was not a passion.

It became even clearer that it wasn't a passion for any of us when the coach would scream at the top of his lungs for the kids to "SIT ON THE BENCH AND HAVE FUN!" They would be reminded at top volume that "BASEBALL IS FUN!" Which Kai was not believing. Neither was I. Neither was Keith. This coach was enthusiastic, but it started to get beyond our level of comfort. We chalked it up to simple differences in level of competitiveness. That's OK, right?

One evening a game lasted into the night. Truly, darkness fell. The air was chilled and the game continued, despite the kids not even being able to see the ball. The umpire approached the coaches to ask for an end to the game. Both coaches on both teams dashed to the plate and had a rather heated exchange with the umpire, both saying that since it was a tie, the players were desperate to play until a win.

I was thinking, these particular coaches had most definitely *not* read or signed the contract. I was also thinking that Newton's Second Law was playing out in a twisted way. In a nutshell, that law states that if you apply the same force to objects of different masses, the resulting acceleration will be different. What I was witnessing was that the force applied to smaller players—forcing them to play way beyond the fun decay curve—was having a greater effect on them than the force acted upon the larger humans involved in this game

It was a weeknight. The kids clearly did *not* care whether or not they had a win. Even the intense ones were done. It was a tie. There was school tomorrow. Keith and I looked around at the other parents for support, but *no parent* near us seemed in agreement with us. They wanted a *win*!

When did *we* become the weird ones? Was there something wrong with us because we didn't have nervous stomachs when the kids played? Was there something out of whack with us because we would rather have Kai tucked into bed with a tied game under his belt than to make tomorrow miserable just to risk the ever-coveted win? Were we uncompetitive softies? Would Kai suffer as an adult, in the modern workplace, for our lack of commitment to this very game?

Maybe, but give the kids their cupcakes and juice boxes, and call it a night! It had already been three hours! There were bats flying around the outfield, for crying out loud—*real* ones!

Finally, the other team hit a home run, and the game was over.

"What a relief!" I said out loud, and looked around to get a nod of agreement; but there were no nods. There was no eye contact, no chuckles, or even responses from the parents nearby. There were crickets.

Beyond twilight, this was the Twilight Zone!

Many of the boys on our team broke down into tears. Kai looked on, then looked at us, wide-eyed. Then one of the coaches informed them, loudly, to look at the other team. They were cheering as if they had won the lottery.

"That's what *winners* look like!" he said to his sniffling team. "*That's* what they look like. *That's* what it looks like to win. Don't *you* want to feel that good? Well, *not tonight*. See you at practice tomorrow." The other coaches seemed embarrassed.

I was stunned. I looked at the other parents. Some were nodding in agreement at the sage wisdom the coach had imparted. My jaw dropped. Kai took his cupcake and joined us.

That night, as I tucked Kai in, he snuggled up with his stuffed wolf, Grayfur, and asked me sleepily, "Mom, why were those kids crying? It was just a game."

"I know it, Honey. I guess it means something more to some people."

"Does that make me a bad ballplayer?"

"Never! Being a good ballplayer means trying your hardest, learning the game, playing, and having fun. Winning is more than scoring."

"I'm not sure about that, Mom. Chad was saying his mother wants him to have all wins because then he can get on All Stars and then he'll have a better chance to be on a good team when he gets older."

"That's a lot of pressure."

"Mom, what's pressure?"

"It's when someone tries to make something really important to you even if it's not."

"Like school?"

"Well, yeah, but get used to *that* pressure. I'm not caving on that. You need your education, Baby. It's the key that unlocks doors."

"Is baseball a key?"

"For some kids, I guess, yes."

"More than school?"

"Well, no—but it's part of the big picture. You get to love whatever you love to do. It could be baseball, it could be horses, it could be surfing, playing ukulele, or raising worms."

"Really, Mom? Worms?"

"You know what I mean. Love what you love. Don't let anyone tell you it's not important. It is. It's who you are. But don't let it make you miserable."

"You mean like that mad coach?"

"Does he seem mad to you?"

"Well, yeah! All the time. He yells *all* the time. His son is on the team, too, and even *he* cries."

Then I saw it. Newton's Second Law, in motion. Kai began to accelerate. The force he had felt did not go unnoticed. Tears erupted, and he gushed.

"So what if I *can't* play baseball as well as Will or Chad? So what if I *can't* catch a grounder? Those things HURT when they hit you! So I *can't* always hit the ball, especially when a kid throws it at your head! And that mad coach *yells* at me and he tells me I'm not *trying,* and so what if I like to dance in the outfield? I hear music. I *like* dancing!"

He sobbed.

The storm passed.

He looked at me.

"You're a great dancer," I said, and bobbed my head with style as I gave myself a backbeat.

Kai laughed. He joined in.

"I hate baseball, Mom."

I couldn't blame him.

"I want to quit."

"Well, don't hate the *sport* because *some* people make it hard. Don't give that power to anyone, even if they are grown-ups and in charge. If it's fun, do it. If not, you can stop after this season. But you can't leave the team. You made a commitment. Finish the season. And remember, there are two sides to everything. That coach might be struggling with some stuff of his own."

"Yeah, he struggles. He struggles to keep calm. Especially around me."

"It's not you, Babe. I know that's really hard to understand. But it's not you. I'll bet that coach maybe played baseball as a kid and was either really, really good or not quite good enough."

"He's *really* good. He can hit the ball out of the park!" Kai's eyes were drooping.

"I know he can, now. But we don't know *why* baseball is so important to him. Let's try to be thoughtful and *let* him be crabby and not let it take *your* power away. Know that when he's yelling at kids next time, that he may actually be yelling at a young version of himself to be better. Maybe *he* was the kid that was chosen last. Maybe his father loved baseball, too, and was really disappointed in him and yelled at him. Maybe that's all he knows. You know? Remember Newton, the scientist and his laws we were talking about? His third law said that for every action there is a reaction. Isn't that cool? So if you and I were on Rollerblades and we were facing each other and pushed each other, we would both move back. The push is the action and the rolling back is the reaction. So maybe this coach was a sweet kid who was only OK at baseball, and his dad yelled, and so now, as a reaction, he yells."

I came up for air. Kai was sound asleep. I didn't blame him. Where the hell was I going with this? Action, reaction, objects, force, motion . . . We're all doing our best. And if we're not—there's a contract out there to keep us in line!

And there's science.

If the ball is going straight—if you love something—then don't let someone else's actions change that path. Stay in motion. But if that ball is still, and there is no passion, don't let anyone's actions push you off your own course—no matter how hard it is to stand up to their power.

Thank you, Isaac Newton.

💡 RUBE GOLDBERG—ACTION AND REACTION

Rube Goldberg (1883–1970) was a Pulitzer Prize–winning cartoonist, sculptor, and author. He's most famous for creating drawings of machines that make the most complicated ways to do a simple task.

WHAT YOU NEED

- Stuff like dominoes, marbles, string, tape, wire, paper, and cardboard
- Space
- Imagination

What You Do

There are no rules. Set things up so that they start an action, and when that action happens, it starts another reaction. For example, roll a baseball down a slanted book into a line of books on end. One knocks into another and so forth and so forth. Each little segment affects the next until you get to the final finish, like having a marble roll into a cup.

IDEAS

- Set up dominoes, or books on end, or DVD cases.
- Bend wire to form a track for a marble to roll along.
- Drip water onto a sponge to weight down one side of a teeter-totter lever.
- Attach one end of a piece of string to your machine and lay the other end on a piece of tape, sticky side up. Roll something over the tape (a roll of duct tape works well) so that the tape sticks to it and carries the string with it, setting the next thing in motion.
- Activate a fan or hair dryer to blow something into place.
- Release a buoyant object under water to allow it to rise up through a series of obstacles.
- Swing a bat into a resting baseball to launch it into the next location.
- Pop a balloon to make space for an object to pass.
- Pop a sand-filled balloon, allowing sand to pour out and change the balance of a lever.

Kai and Leo have a Rube Goldberg bag that has string, sponges, dominoes, marbles, baseballs, blocks, wire, and all manner of stuff to put together an elaborate machine. It's an awesome way to show action and reaction and inertia. It's a Newton fest!

24

THE SPARK INSIDE

KONA WAS MY FIRST BABY: a beautiful collie/shepherd mix rescue that we adopted when we were pregnant-but-didn't-know-it-yet with Kai. I spied her when Keith when I went to the local shelter to donate towels.

I offhandedly told Keith, "I'm just going back there to look at the animals."

"No way, Honey! You won't just look. I know you!"

"I'm just going to *look*! Don't worry."

"Don't worry, she says," Keith grumbled to the receptionist as I wandered through the door that led to the animals.

I saw cute dog after cute dog looking forlornly through their chain-link doors. I cooed. I clucked. I tried to comfort them; but I walked on—until I saw Kona.

Only she wasn't Kona yet. She was Shasta. That was the name they had assigned. I made eye contact with her, and there was this spark. I just knew.

When Keith came back a few minutes later, he saw me clinging to the front of her cage.

"Honey, this is our dog," I said.

"Oh no, really?"

"Look at her."

We looked at her sad and wary eyes. He pretended to complain, but Keith ultimately agreed; there was a spark there.

"Maybe we could let her out to see her?" Keith suggested.

Twenty minutes later, we were driving home with our new dog.

Kona was my constant companion. My shadow. She followed me everywhere. She walked at my heels through the woods when I walked every day. She welcomed Keith home with wags and licks, and when Kai was born she appointed herself his personal guardian. She ushered us through many firsts.

She weathered the addition of two kittens. She monitored them, making sure they did no permanent damage. She kept intruders off the lawn, out of the house, and away from the garden.

Kona saw our family through the move to the "country." She delighted in never needing a leash and never strayed from the yard. She had her favorite spot under the maple tree. Sometimes shaded, sometimes sunny, it was the perfect place to watch all the goings-on in the yard. She barked encouragingly and trotted alongside the boys when they learned to ride their bikes, when they tried Rollerblades for the first time, when they scootered, and when they skateboarded.

She joined in every water fight and waited patiently when I watered the garden. She allowed us to dress her up for Halloween. She let the boys roll all over her. She played fetch. She let us know when there were raccoons, deer, and coyotes about.

When I wrote, she slept happily under my desk.

She was wonderful.

When my parents moved from Maine, it's as if Kona knew my mom was battling something. She shadowed Mom wherever she went. She snuggled with her on the couch. I have read about how some animals might smell subtle chemical changes in people with sicknesses, but that doesn't explain why Kona stayed with Mom when she began to wander deeper into her Alzheimer's. She calmed Mom when she forgot where she was, just by being present. For some reason, Mom connected with

Kona. She saw the spark. Kona never forgot her. Mom would talk and talk to Kona when no one was in the room.

Having good friends who happen to be veterinarians is a handy thing. One summer afternoon Liz, Kona, and I watched the kids running through the sprinkler. Kai was six, Kati was five, and Leo was four. Their delighted screeching filled the warm afternoon. The sunlight dappled the lawn. All was well with the world. Kona lay on her side and I stretched next to her, patting her.

I noticed a lump.

Liz trotted to her car, grabbed her bag, and aspirated the lump on the spot. Both of us had a bad feeling. It was the first of many.

Kona had breast cancer. Over the next year, she had it removed—twice. Then there was a blockage in her intestine, which we removed. She never recovered. She dwindled. I couldn't see it, because I didn't want to see it.

I tried everything. I made poached chicken breasts to entice her to eat, and she did eat, but haltingly. I realized that she wasn't doing it for her; she was doing it for me. I released her from eating, and she curled up in her bed. Coiled into a fuzzy ball, with one eye on me—as always, she stayed there.

Liz came over. The first thing she said was, "Poor thing. That dog looks like she's exhausted."

I sobbed.

The last thing I wanted to do was be that person who kept an animal alive because of my selfish desire not to let go. She was in pain. She would not recover. She was dying.

That afternoon, we prepared to say good-bye. Liz would come to us, and the whole procedure would be painless and as comforting to Kona as possible.

Kai and Leo really couldn't grasp what was happening. They knew I was sad. They knew Kona was going away. Yet they patted her perkily, and said "Bye, Kona!" quickly, and ran off to play.

Letting her go was physically painful. We put her on her favorite bed, in her favorite spot in the yard—under the maple—and patted her. She was calm. She put her head on my lap. She knew how much she was loved. Liz sedated her. She fell asleep, and then Liz administered the drug that stopped the suffering. I watched her go.

When she died, I was crushed.

Kai and Leo comforted me, and Leo, who was four at the time, whispered, "Mommy, now can we get a cheetah?"

Kai chided him. "LEO! We can't get a *cheetah*; but maybe we could get a corgi, Mom?"

I did that laughing/crying thing, which I think probably scared them.

"Mom, why are you crying?"

"I miss Kona, Sweetie. I loved her so much."

"Please stop crying, Mommy!" Leo said, starting to tear up.

"Oh, Honey. I know how hard it is to see someone you love crying. When you love deeply, you hurt greatly at the end. But even if it makes you feel uncomfortable, it's a normal, healthy thing to do in this situation. It gets out the feeling of loss. It starts the process of healing after someone dies."

"You still love her, right?" Kai asked.

"Yes, I do."

"So she's kind of still here, right?"

"I guess you're right."

"Does that make her undead, like a zombie?"

"Not exactly."

"Is she an angel?" asked Kai.

"Maybe."

"A ghost?" asked Leo.

"Maybe, poetically. Nobody knows what happens after you die."

"Mommy, what does it mean to die?" Leo asked while still petting the cooling body of what was Kona.

"Well, it means that the body stops working. The lungs don't breathe air anymore. The heart doesn't pump blood anymore, and the brain isn't sending any more signals to the muscles. The body is worn out. It stops."

"So what will happen to her body?"

"When something dies, all the systems stop working. Circulation, respiratory, digestion, nervous systems . . ."

"OK."

"Also, the immune system. That's the system that keeps invading critters like viruses and bacteria from taking over and making you sick. There are loads of these bugs around that want to use your body to make more copies of themselves. When you are alive, the immune system shuts the invaders down before they can make you sick.

"But when something dies, the immune system stops working, too. So the doorway is wide open. Bacteria and microbes come in, make themselves at home, and start the party. It doesn't take long—only a few weeks—for these things to completely take the body apart, cell by cell, and carry it away."

"Everything?"

"Not the skeleton. That's made out of hard minerals and it doesn't get carted away."

"Kind of like our memories."

"Absolutely."

"But what about *Kona*?"

"What do you mean, Honey?"

"What happens to the *real* her?"

"Well, there's that spark inside that makes someone who they are. It's what makes you you, it makes me me, and no one knows what happens to that spark when the body dies."

"Does it get carried away by bacteria?"

"I don't think so. I don't know for sure, but I think it's like light. It's a different kind of energy, and it goes somewhere. Where? I don't really know."

"Are you going to die, Mom?"

"I am. Someday. Not today. Everyone dies one day."

"OK, Mom. Bye! Come on, Leo. Let's ride bikes. Bye, Kona."

Then they were off with their bike and trike to conquer the driveway.

Liz and Keith took Kona away, and I watched the boys playing from Kona's spot. They pedaled lightning fast and negotiated turns to avoid ants and rocks. The sun glinted off their fenders.

"Mom!" Kai screamed.

Oh no! I dried my tears. Sobered out of grief by fear, I ran over to him. "What, Honey?"

He was not bleeding. He was not crying. He was smiling and pointing.

"Look! It's Kona."

The observation froze me to the spot. He was pointing to the sunlight that was reflecting off the shiny handlebars of his new bike. The light danced across the bushes and the grass.

"Oh, Honey, that's the sunlight bouncing off your handlebars. It bumps up against something shiny and bounces back."

"Yup. I know. It's Kona—it's the light! She would be running around with us if she still had her body. Now she's just light, and she's still here."

He pedaled off.

The next day, we made a mobile out of small mirrors, sea glass, and Kona's dog tags. We hung it on a branch of the maple tree, where it still dangles to this day. Sometimes the sunlight catches it. Sometimes my headlights catch it when I drive in at night. Every time it does, I see the light dance across the yard, and Kona's with me again.

THE DANCING SPARK MOBILE

Make a light-refracting outdoor garden mobile that can make light dance across the yard.

WHAT YOU NEED

- A wooden or metal ring (for the top of the mobile—we used a metal ring from the lid of a jam jar)
- 1-inch craft mirrors (you can get these in craft stores)
- Beads or crystals
- Any special items you want to include (we used Kona's dog tags)
- Soft monofilament line
- Superglue
- Packing tape (or other easily removable tape)

What You Do

1. Decide how many strands you want hanging down. We did only one, but you can do as many as you want. Cut the monofilament in 3-foot pieces for as many strands as you like.
2. Organize your pieces—beads and mirrors—into a pattern you like.
3. Thread the first bead on your line—this will be the bottom piece. Thread the line through the bead three or four times to secure the bead in place. Tie a knot and put a dot of superglue on the bead and the line to keep it snug.
4. Thread more beads if you like. Thread the line and dot it with superglue to secure the beads.
5. Attach the mirrors. Place a mirror face down and lay the monofilament across. Dab it with superglue and place a second mirror face up, sandwiching the line securely in between the mirrors. Let it dry.
6. When everything is dry, tie the top of the filament to the ring.
7. Hang your mobile where it can catch the light.

25

SUCKING THE BOUNCE

I CAN'T JUMP on the trampoline with my kids anymore.

Hell, I know it's not even safe to let them do it in the first place; but there it is. I think the plusses outweigh the minuses.

Our trampoline, also known as a huge "attractive nuisance," sits in the backyard right next to the awesome zip line Keith put in when he turned fifty. (Is there a correlation? Maybe.) Anyway, the trampoline has enabled my guys (and myself) to bounce-bounce-bounce in the loveliest of ways. It's just wonderful to use that potential energy and transfer of energy to get so high in the air. God bless you, Isaac Newton!

"Mommy, Mommy, *bounce* with us, PLEASE!" Kai and Leo plead in tandem.

At first I thought it was because they just *loved* being with me and playing together. I cherish these moments, because as they get older, I know it's only a matter of time before they won't be able to handle the embarrassment of seeing their mother on the trampoline.

"Of course!" I say. No matter what I was doing, I would drop it and bounce. It's fun! And not without side benefits. My aerobic capacity has increased, and my legs are downright steely.

It took me awhile to realize what was *really* going on.

Leo's agenda was to perfect his flips, twists, and other acrobatics. My job was to sit on the trampoline and watch him twist and spin through the air and then attempt my own version of "flipping," which was a baby roll. Sad but elegant in its way. Leo utilized my efforts as a benchmark of comparison to which his own stunts reflected like gold.

Anyone would look like an Olympian next to me. I was happy to serve my role.

While Leo perfected his gymnastics and his confidence, Kai was working some serious physics.

"Mom?"

"Yes, Honey?"

"How does the trampoline make me bounce so high?"

"How do you think it might work?"

"I bounce down and it bounces me back up?"

"Exactly. Look, there's a frame made of metal and all these springs. Then there's the stretchy fabric. That's a trampoline. Bounce down on it and you are loading this thing with energy. The springs stretch out and are loaded with power. When they snap back, they pull the fabric tight, and all the energy you put in with your jump flings you right back into the air."

"So a big bounce makes me fly higher?"

"Yup."

"And the more I weigh, the bigger the bounce?"

"Yup. The harder you push down on the trampoline, the more energy is stored, the more powerful the snap back will be that will send you soaring through the air—"

"Come on Mom, BOUNCE!"

We did; but suddenly I was no longer sailing joyfully into the air. I was bouncing and working hard, but getting no lift. Kai, on the other hand, was flying higher than ever. He was figuring out how to jump at the exact spot and time to suck the energy from my considerable bounce and use it to fling himself sky high.

It was brilliant and exciting. It was also physically deflating and exhausting for me. My jumps were no longer high flying, but Kai's were off the charts. We would go on like that for a time, and then I would collapse in a heap on the trampoline. Kai would join me and we'd look up into the trees overhead. One of us having sucked the bounce, the other sucking wind.

"I go SOOO high when I bounce with you!"

"Yup." Pant. Pant. "Technically, the entire total of your energy is made up of the moving energy called kinetic energy plus the stored-in-the-springs energy—your potential energy."

I may make a huge bounce and only be capable of a baby roll, but I could still pull my weight with science at least!

"Mommy, you have a LOT of stored energy!"

What mother wouldn't love to hear that?

"Thanks, Honey."

Kai was up and bouncing. Ready to make more experiments.

The fact that Kai used *my* energy to fly higher was a metaphor I could understand. It was beautiful in its way, but kind of frustrating. I still wanted the air.

Hell, I needed the air at that moment. I lay flat on the trampoline as Kai bounced. I breathed deeply. Still gasping. It was all I could do to keep up with my boys, but to launch them to new heights was exhausting my resources.

I gazed up into the air. It was late summer. The light slanted through the pine trees, and the air itself was dotted with dandelion fluff, tree fuzz, and various tiny seeds and spores. It dawned on me that this trampoline dance of ours was more than just a metaphor for the energy that we put into parenting; it was a symbol for the nature of all things. Parents of all sorts stand up to launch their offspring—from the top of the heap right down to the bottom dwellers—as best they can into the world. It wasn't just me. It was the throbbing life on the planet, all doing the same thing.

Ponder, as I did prone on the trampoline, the microscopic dung-loving fungi (called coprophilous—if you must know). It's not an elegant job they provide but a necessary one. If not for microbes like these, we'd be up to our eyeballs in cow dung, horse dung, llama dung, and any other array of friendly herbivore dung. Not good.

The mature fungi have a challenge. In order to survive, they need to make sure their spores are eaten by the herbivores that produce the dung. It's their circle of life. Think about that the next time you're having a rough day. Spore into the cow—fungus pooped out.

Here's the thing—even the dimmest herbivore knows not to graze near where it poops. Since poop is where the fungus lives, and it doesn't have any legs to move around with, that makes it tough for a fungus to get its spores far enough away and into the path of a hungry herbivore. Its job is to make sure its spores are going to be eaten.

So these fungi have developed ways to really launch their spores out into the world: the stalks that grow out of the dung swell with fluid. The spore is perched on top. The fungus matures. It measures about 1/20 of an inch tall. The fluid builds up at the end and then BLAMMO—it explodes, shooting the spore at speeds of thirty-five feet per second! That's the fastest recorded flight in nature! The spore gets height as well, reaching peaks of over six feet and landing eight feet away from the parent fungus. Technically the fungus can launch its seed over a cow from a dung pile to a patch of tasty grass in the blink of an eye. The mature fungus then collapses. Its job is done. Energy expended. Spore launched.

The irony is not lost on me.

Our boys were experimenting and staring down limitations of physical and epic proportions. It synced up perfectly with the beginning of the bittersweet journey into separation and identity, puberty, and beyond.

Kai and Leo needed me now. I was helping to load their springs. I know it won't be long before they dazzle the world with the flips and heights they'll reach on their own.

MEGA BOUNCE

Use a basketball and a tennis ball to bounce the tennis ball higher than the roof.

WHAT YOU NEED

- A basketball
- A tennis ball

What You Do

1. Hold the basketball at shoulder height, and with your other hand, hold the tennis ball directly on top of the basketball.
2. Drop both balls at the same time.
3. The tennis ball should bounce off the charts!

WHAT'S GOING ON?

The basketball hits the ground, but that's not all. The ground also hits the basketball, giving it the energy for a "bounce." The basketball is way heavier than the tennis ball, so it's got a lot more energy in its bounce. With the tennis ball on top of the basketball, the basketball hits the ground, it bounces back up, and hits the tennis ball. So now some of the basketball's energy gets transferred to the tennis ball. It may not be much to the basketball, but to the tennis ball, it's a huge amount of energy. The basketball kind of flops. It doesn't bounce high at all. But the tennis ball bounces super high! It gets launched! It's all about energy transfer!

ACKNOWLEDGMENTS

Oh, this is like winning an Oscar! I would like to thank my agent . . . No really. I *would* like to thank my agent, Joy Tutela, whom I adore. She has endured and cultivated my persistent-camper self and believed in me from the get-go. For an insecure writer like me, that's priceless.

I would also like to thank my lovely, kind, and insightful editor, Jenn Urban-Brown, and all the folks at Roost—Steven Pomije, Kate Levy, Julie Saidenberg, and Julia Gaviria—who helped make this book.

Thanks also to my writing family: Mary Cushman, Megan Drew, Tina Cachules, Warren Read, Susan Goodwin-Thomas, Dinah Manoff, Suzanne Selfors, and Jim Brunelle. Their comments, enthusiasm, and skills helped polish this diamond in the rough.

Thank you, Garth, Ian, Susan, Fred, and all the science lovers out there.

Jill, Amy, Sabina, Cindy, Debbie, Liz, Sherri, Rose, Kristina, Angie, Maura, Maria, Marion, Trang, Shana, Leslie, Susan, Colleen, Toshi—and all the Moms extraordinaire who inspire me every day. Especially my own mama, Ellen.

Thanks to Dad, to Bill, and to Meg. I couldn't have even done this without you.

And of course thanks to Keith and Kai and Leo—my raisons d'être.

ABOUT THE AUTHOR

LYNN BRUNELLE is an Emmy Award–winning television writer for *Bill Nye, the Science Guy* and a best-selling author/illustrator. She lives in the Pacific Northwest with her husband, children, and small menagerie of dogs, cats, fish, and various wild things that pass through.

TASHA VANASSE